THE LOGIC OF INVENTION

THE LOGIC OF INVENTION

by Roy Wagner

Hau Books
Chicago

Cover and layout design: Sheehan Moore
Figures and illustrations: Roy Wagner

Editorial office: Michelle Beckett, Justin Dyer, Sheehan Moore, Faun Rice,
and Ian Tuttle

Typesetting: Prepress Plus (www.prepressplus.in)

ISBN: 978-0-9991570-5-3
LCCN: 2018963544

Hau Books
Chicago Distribution Center
11030 S. Langley
Chicago, IL 60628
www.haubooks.com

Hau Books is printed, marketed, and distributed by The University of Chicago Press.
www.press.uchicago.edu

Printed in the United States of America on acid-free paper.

To DONNA MARIE HAYES, soulmate

Table of Contents

List of figures and illustrations   ix
A note from the editor   xi
Preface and abstract of the argument   xiii
Acknowledgments   xix

CHAPTER 1
The reciprocity of perspectives   1

CHAPTER 2
Facts picture us to themselves: Wittgenstein's propositions   19

CHAPTER 3
Nonlinear causality   59

CHAPTER 4
The ontology of representation   89

Epilogue: Totality viewed in the imagination   113

References   121

List of figures and illustrations

Binary involution in the Mayan Long Count   13
Synthesis: Retroactive conception   69
Antisynthesis: Proactive Mythmaking ("Creation")   73
Telefolip—A "Western" perspective   80
Dimensional co-dependency   91
Third point perspective   92
Triasmus   101
Denmark: Royal incest   108
Bee-mark: Royal outcest   110
Totality viewed in the imagination   119

A note from the editor

The Logic of Invention is a posthumous publication. The editing of the manuscript attempted to preserve the text as close as possible to the author's last available draft and creative impulse. His was a great mind gifted in joining and differentiating the multifarious flows of human vitality.

Godspeed, analogic man.

Preface and abstract of the argument

What makes anthropology distinctive is that it is neither a subjective nor an objective discipline, but rather one that makes its whole contribution to knowledge by tracking and enhancing the transformation between subject and object. The transformation can go either way, but for convenience I shall call it the subject/object shift. Basically, everything we think, do, or say depends on the ambiguity between subject and object, redefined syntactically as "subject" and "predicate," pragmatically as "means" and "ends," aesthetically as "figure" and "ground," and so forth. How these different contextual variants differ from one another is a measure of how they are the same, and vice versa, and so we can generalize by using a double-proportional comparison—between difference and similarity, on one hand, and subject and object, on the other: *the subject is the difference between itself and the object; the object is the similarity between them*. Note that this make the subject a self-differentiating variable, relative and object-dependent, just as the "subjective" is apprehended in psychology. Viewed in another way, this double comparison also serves as the figure/field inversion of perception itself: time is the difference between itself and space; space is the similarity between the two. Hence (*pace* Einstein) the nature of perception itself forbids a conflation of space and time as a single continuum.

This book is about the many subvariants of the subject/object transformation, some of them very familiar to a modern reading audience, like figure–ground reversal, the mirror-reflection ego (Lacan), the self-recursive structure of the aphorism, the reciprocity of perspectives, and the double-proportional comparison itself ("using two words twice and in reverse order the second time").

Others, like the self-recursive inversion of ends and means (e.g., what Gregory Bateson called the cybernetic feedback loop, and the practiced art of chiasmatic rhetoric that the Daribi of Papua New Guinea call "the talk that turns back on itself as it is spoken"), much less so.

Let me start with the false familiarity of mirrors as Jacques Lacan and Louis XIV did. Just what, exactly, did Louis mean by "l'état c'est moi": was it the false familiarity of his mirror-reflection ego, or the true unfamiliarity of the mirror people who haunted the Galerie des Glaces? Pay close attention to this double comparison: "The one in the mirror borrows the action of looking to see itself" (Wagner 2001: 234). Just who, in this statement, is familiar and who is not? "When you look into a pool of water or a mirror," an Angan speaker from Papua New Guinea once told me, "the one you see there is not you, and it is not human." Seventeenth-century France was ruled by impostors, who basked in the reflected glory of others and whose actual substance was effectively one photon thick. But the reciprocity of perspective is the definition of power itself, the self-modeling focus of human sentience, the transposition of ends and means, the fact that the mirror turns its reflection of you into your reflection of it. The Vicomte des Glaces whom you see in the mirror borrows your eye to see himself through you. Upon further reflection, then, cars drive their drivers, machines run the machinist, and, as chapter 2 confidently asserts, "facts picture *us* to *themselves*."

These are what a linguist would call ergative (deriving from the Greek word for "energy") usages, and the logic behind them is that of subject/object inversion, just as in the mirror-view of oneself. What is illustrated here is the well-proven fact that it is impossible to perceive energy directly; its presence can only be detected through its effects on other things. (In other words energy, like your own face, is the most familiar thing in your whole environmental surround, yet neither can be observed save by reflection.) When we speak of the energy of a machine or even a whole technology, we are not speaking of energy at all, but rather of its reflection in the machine or technology itself. The machine or the technology is merely a way of objectifying something that otherwise would have only a felt, or subjective, presence for our senses. (This poses a major problem in particle physics, for figures of speech like neutrino, photon, gauge boson, etc., are neither parts nor wholes in and of themselves, but in-between surrogates for what Victor Turner would call "liminality," and Werner Heisenberg "indeterminacy.")

Such ad hoc objectifications are not natural phenomena at all; they do not represent the thing to be explained or understood, but only the means of explaining or understanding it. Thus they do not represent something that an idealist might call "nature," but only the steps that must be taken in order to recognize nature as a viable subject of study. Therefore what I have called here a "subject/object shift" is in reality a transposition of ends and means, and thus a variant form of the double-proportional comparison (in this case: the nature of culture is the culture of nature).

What does all of this mean when translated into the language of the layperson? It means that energy and liminality share the same description, and because two things equal to the same thing are also equal to one another, there is no tangible or even conceptual difference between them. Energy and liminality are indistinguishable from one another. Both are invisible to the practiced eye, and their presence or action must be inferred from circumstantial evidence.

Liminal expressions—forms of articulation like metaphors and aphorisms—that operate only through their own self-generated chiasmus, synthesize the only aspect of language wherein the energy of meaningfulness is generated and conveyed. This is what the Daribi people of Papua New Guinea mean when they call their chiasmatic power-talk "the speech of remote intentions" (the literal significance of their word *porigi*: "What makes a man a big man; is it having more wives and pigs than others?" "If a man can talk *porigi* well, he gets all the wives and pigs he needs."). Language itself, with all of its phonologies, grammars, lexicons, and syntax, is only an enabling factor for the energy that constitutes the main argument of human speech, quite literally as "speech of remote intentions." Only in this way can we deal with the fact that some books absorb the energies of the reader, whereas others reenergize them. Think twice before you say "that is a very absorbing book."

What does this, in turn, really mean? It means that there is an energy of saying things that is entirely separate and distinct from what is said, and the grammatical or syntactical correlates of saying it that way. The poet Dylan Thomas was a complete master of this technique:

Though wise men at their end know dark is right
because their words had forked no lightning, they
do not go gentle into that good night.
(*Do not go gentle into that good night*, by Dylan Thomas)

Like the exchange of life breath between human beings, which it closely mimics, the energy of saying things has nothing to do with communication or "information exchange," and is far older than *Homo sapiens*. Should the simile be allowed, the energy of saying things is more like a disembodied form of body language, or like the saying that "a metaphor is two words, each dividing the significance of the other between them." (Warning: do not try this in your basement or garage; one of you is likely to get pregnant.)

The bottom line on meaning and self-expression, and the key issue insofar as the reciprocity of perspectives is concerned, is the nature and intent of metaphor (trope). The big mistake is to imagine that metaphor (verbal imagery) is somehow adventitious, a thing in and of itself, and thus adjunctive to language. It is not! It *is* language. It is not "about" something called "the imagination," but rather the imagination, whatever that might be, *is about it*. What that means, in the light of this discussion, is that the thing we have been calling "language" is both tool and user at once, more or less like the human hand, and that the thing we call "metaphor" is the automatic reflex of its reinversion out of itself.

This means that metaphor, in the final analysis, "is born of the attempt to get rid of metaphor, and survives as the boundary condition of our inability to do so" (Wagner 2001: 20). It means that metaphor is the self-sustaining basis of the reciprocity of perspectives in that it defines the ultimate transposition of ends and means, for it "works the way it means and means the way it works" (Wagner 2001: 34).

The ultimate objective of this discussion is to guide the reader through the transition from the chiasmatic logic of twentieth-century philosophers like Bertrand Russell, Ludwig Wittgenstein, and Kurt Gödel to the third-point perspective of obviation, the logic of the "triasmus" with its event horizon. In more conventional terms, the transition encompasses a transposing of ends and means between the chiasmatic self-resonance of two inverse analogies reinforcing one another, and the self-abnegation of the chiasmus divided by itself in the realization of what I have called "obviation," the dialectical self-closure beyond which no further action can take place, which I have likened to the astrophysical "event horizon" of the black hole. In this sense one might call the operation that I am describing here "the logical end of logic."

A logical operation that divides itself by itself, like a fractal equation in mathematics, can be understood as a self-modeling one, and the best evidence for this is the self-inverting triangular format of the obviation diagram itself, based on the classic "Sierpinski grid" or "Sierpinski gasket" of fractal mathematics.

By the same token, the fact that every point or meaningful juncture on the obviation triangle is modeled in the same proportional relation to the others as those others are to it means that there is no privileged linear order or chrono-logical sequency in their mutual arrangement, so that a single order of prec-edence, such as the traditional linear cause-and-effect model, is less effective in expressing the mutual contiguity of the points than a nonlinear one. Hence self-modeling and nonlinear causality are not only concomitant features of one another, but diagnostic features of obviation itself.

Taking a cue from Lévi-Strauss's original Canonic Formula for Myth (cf. *The raw and the cooked*), we might speak of them as harmonic, and follow my colleague Mark Sicoli in treating their mutual self-reinforcement as the energizing effect of resonance. That the energic qualities of music are chiasmatic rather than causal is aptly demonstrated by the fact that most of the technical features of musical expression, such as counterpoint or syncopation, are chiastic rather than linear. So perhaps Lévi-Strauss was right after all: the image con-veyed in a metaphor is acoustic rather than visual.

On a broader scale, one that is intrinsic to the evolution of sentience itself, the best term for the phenomenon I am describing here would not be "chiasmatic logic" nor even "the second attention," but simply resonance. Usually identified with communication or navigation in orders like the chiroptera (cf. Wagner 2001) or cetaceans, resonance is also their medium of creative self-expression. In that sense the most definitive step in the evolution of "Man the Musician," as Victor Zuckerkandl (1973) calls us, would be the lowering of the larynx in the throat, which took place roughly 250,000 years ago. After all, it was my resonance that wrote these pages, and yours that is reading them.

Acknowledgments

My debt to Giovanni da Col is profound; without his generous support and wise encouragement this book would never have seen the light of day. I also owe my heartfelt thanks to a brilliant young scholar, Theodoros Kyriakides, whose almost intuitive grasp of the subject matter helped immensely during the constant rewriting of chapter 1. I am also indebted to my ever-wise mentor, Dame Marilyn Strathern, and to Martin Holbraad, Morten Pedersen, and Alberto Corsín Jiménez for their keen insights into obviation as a theoretical agenda, to my colleague Mark Sicoli for his ingenious insights into resonance as a linguistic motivator, and to my friends Yale Landsberg and Stephen Paul King. My special thanks as well to Karen Hall and Mildred Dean for their help in preparing this manuscript.

CHAPTER I

The reciprocity of perspectives

"Imagine a tree whose top foliage cuts the shape of a human face against the sky," say the Tolai people of East New Britain, in Papua New Guinea, "and fix the shape of that face in your mind, so that it appears as a real face, and not just a profile. When you have finished, go back to the tree, and visualize it as a free-standing object without reference to the face. When you have both images firmly fixed in your mind, just hold them in suspension and keep shifting your attention from one to the other: tree/face, face/tree, tree/face, and so on."

"That is what we call a *tabapot*. Man is a *tabapot*. For you see the human being is encased within the boundaries of their own body, but they want what is outside of their own body. But when they get what is outside of their own body, they want to be encased back in the body again."

Somewhat taken aback by what appeared to be one of the best definitions of human being I had ever heard, I told the story to my Barok congeners in New Ireland and asked them whether they had anything like *tabapot* in their own tradition.

"Yes we do," they replied, "we call it *pire wuo*," a term that means literally "the reciprocity of perspectives," or perhaps "the exchange of viewpoints." "That," they went on to say, "is how you put power in art."

They were referring, apparently, to the techniques of color-inversion, self-inverting geometric patterning, and other forms of figure–field inversion that are characteristic of what we unknowingly refer to as "tribal" or "primitive" art. But they could as well have been discussing the closely related trick of perspectival figure–ground reversal used by Western painters to create the illusion of depth in a painting—the exchange of viewpoints between foreground and background, the secret of projective geometry.

But this purely optical effect, known as *trompe l'oeil* or "fooling the eye" to art historians, is a far cry from what Barok mean by "putting power in art." For them, as for M. C. Escher, the "depth" is three-dimensional and holographic, as evidenced in the primarily architectural iconography of the Barok ritual feasting complex. Ritual perspectives are not simply represented or portrayed, but actually "brought to life" by performing self-legitimating ritual actions within a three-dimensional theater-space, much as we would do in staging a Shakespeare play. The point is clear, for regardless of whether talking about the illusion of depth or the depth of the illusion itself, we do not live in the *real* world, whatever that might mean, but instead live our lives as a *represents* of that world.

The tactical application of the reciprocity of perspectives, belonging as it does to the formal paradigm of the double-proportional comparison, represents an entire world of experience in and of itself. Like Freud's subconscious, the self-isolated Dreaming of the Australian Aborigines, and the Meso-American second attention, made up entirely of contradictory propositions, it is based entirely upon analogy, metaphor, and chiasmatic combinations thereof, and integrates the same syllogistic patterning as Gödel's Proof.

Hence, one might say, the reciprocity of perspectives is written into the constitution of the human species as its primal phenomenon—that is, it is not a purely mental or symbolic artifact, but an evolutionary achievement, like the upright posture or the lowered larynx. This is the principle of antitwinning (Wagner 2001: chap. 4), the evolutionary fact that the generic human organism is modeled upon itself in two distinctive ways, each one countervening the other. Gender is twinned outward from the basic human form into two distinctive body types called "male" and "female," whereas laterality, the "sides" of the body or right/left coordinates, is twinned inward to meet at the body's longitudinal centerfold to form the single individual organism. So much may be intuited immediately from everyday experience, but it is not the whole story. For we are artificial as well as natural organisms, and we model ourselves in two opposite ways at once: we are our own analogy for ourselves, creating a double-proportional paradox, a transmutation of ends and means, by inverting the two kinds of inwardness and outwardness upon each other. So, to demonstrate the role of the subject/object shift in this, the human constitution as a whole, it is necessary to include the obverse mode of antitwinning as well. This is the fact that in the obverse mode, it is gender that is twinned inward, whereas laterality is twinned outward.

Hence the species models itself upon itself in counterintuitive terms, for what we get in the obversive mode is what we would otherwise call an artificial (e.g., "cultural") rather than a natural ontology. For gender turned inward upon itself is incest, whose objectification as such forms the basis for the deliberate recognition of kinship as such, whereas the outward twinning of laterality through the external extensions of hands and feet forms the basis of tool making, tool use, and technology, for the crafting of artifacts that are external to the body. This point is highly significant, since it demonstrates that kin relations and technology, otherwise considered to be adventitious or accidental "discoveries," are in fact given properties of our human constitution and, as the Tolai example suggests, direct consequences of the reciprocity of perspectives, what it means to be human in the species's own terms.

This in turn sheds some light on Jacques Lacan's brilliant observation that the subconscious is language, meaning that language, too, is chiasmatic and self-recursive in its very conception, a dispensation of antitwinning and the double-proportional comparison. As Ludwig Wittgenstein put it in Proposition 4.121 of the *Tractatus* (1961): "What finds its reflection in language, language cannot represent." In other words, like the commonplace wheel, and like the reciprocity of perspectives itself, the cognitive basis of language itself is not too complex, but too simple, to understand. What does this really mean? It means that the complexity that we associate with ordinary scientific or rationalist explanation—the rationalization of the scientific object—conceals rather than reveals the subject/object shift that is entailed in all double-comparative, or analogical, thinking. As Henry David Thoreau put it in his journal entry for September 3, 1851: "All perception of truth is the detection of an analogy" ([1851] 1993: 201). Thus, by analogy with that analogy, one might liken the self-replicating but also self-contradictory counterposition of the antitwins to the action of a moving wheel, showing that whichever way the wheel may be bisected—top to bottom, front to rear, and even in the extreme case center to periphery—exactly half of the wheel is moving in a direction opposite to that of the other, but with the same speed and momentum. Hence, for instance, the absolute center of the wheel is completely motionless, whereas the outer periphery expresses the full effective compass of its motion, yet regardless of this fact, both share the same speed and momentum.

Nothing but counterintuitive effects of this sort can explain the classic anthropological conviction that humanity at large is obsessed with dichotomies and/or dualities, though in every case these turn out to be projections of the double-proportional comparison. Thus the ancient Egyptians, who called their country "The Two Lands," included in that term all the different oppositions that serve to make it distinctive. And the ancient Mayans, who called their vision of the universe "this world of dualities," actually derived their whole world order from the serial permutations and combinations of the Antitwins, identified in the Popol Vuh as "The Hero Twins."

It was, however, the ancient Toltecs of highland Mexico, with their concept of the "doubling" of the energy body with the physical body, who conceived of the basic antitwinning principle in terms of the self-inversional properties of the mirror-reflection. In that sense the one you see in the mirror is the antitwin of the physical organism that is looking into it, for the shape and surroundings of the latter are inverted laterally (left to right and back to front), but not longitudinally (top to bottom), basically allowing the axis of human manipulation to be viewed at an obverse angle. But, far from being the mere curiosity that it is for us, this property was identified as the most potent weapon in the sociopolitical arena, called Tezcatlipoca, or "The Smoking Mirror."

A double-reflecting surface including a layer of polished obsidian glass, the Toltec understood it as a kind of doorway connecting the world of the energy beings (Castaneda's "inorganic awarenesses") with our own, and in effect articulating antitwinning as an agency that can act freely—of its own accord. It is as though the energy being or "ally" that obtains its whole sense of being from its reflection in ours became active in the world in the form of the four Tezcatlipoca Brothers, manifesting the four cardinal directions, as though Lacan's mirror-reflection ego were elevated to divine status.

What we have taken for granted as an all-important distinction between nature and culture, between phenomena as they really exist in the world, on one hand, and how we use them and make sense of them, on the other, is not so much a matter of human categorization or symbolization as it is an overt acknowledgment of the subject/object shift. It is a matter of nonlinear, rather than linear, causality. On this understanding, it is the shift itself that is the phenomenon, and not its point of application to empirical reality. The shift is simply a shift from subject to object, or object to subject, without regard to the particulars of the situation.

Let me validate this point, as well as the one before it, by making a deliberate and self-conscious shift from the conceptual to the physical. The concept of energy is impossible to define, witness, or implement without taking the subject/object shift and its incumbent reciprocity of perspectives into account. No shift/no energy. In other words, in spite of our conjectures to the contrary, and in spite of a tradition that sees "energy" as something that can be generated, transmitted, used, or stored, energy exists nowhere in the worlds of conjecture or reality except for those points at which "it" undergoes a transformation from one "kind" to another. Even in seeing we transform the photonic energy of visible light into the neuronic energy of the optic nerve, but that only goes to show that there is no such thing as photonic energy or neuronic energy: there is only the point-event of their transformation. To put it more bluntly, there are no specific "kinds" of energy except for the generic "kind" of its transformation from one specific kind to another. So we are really talking about names here, rather than physical states, and the names register a continuum that is scale-invariant, which means that the transformation keeps its scale regardless of size or complexity. It is the cosmos as well as the metrics we use to gauge its significance, as in the observation that space is "the only kind of time that is still around, and that really *matters*" (Wagner 2001: 254). In other words, the so-called "space-time continuum" is neither space, nor time, nor even a continuum, but another victim of the double-proportional comparison, for when viewed as a subject it turns into an object, and when viewed as an object, it becomes a subject.

It stands to reason, then, that just as the "energy physics" of the early twentieth century was dominated almost exclusively by the double-proportional comparison and its incumbent subject/object shift, so its respective microcosmic and macrocosmic expressions, Heisenberg's Indeterminacy Principle and Einstein's Relativity Principle, will contrast with one another on the same basis.

For all the controversy that surrounded this issue, much of it in the debates between Niels Bohr and Albert Einstein ("God does not play dice," etc.), the double-proportional comparison between Heisenberg's Indeterminacy Principle, for which he was awarded the Nobel Prize in 1932, and Einstein's Principle of General Relativity, mention of which was conspicuously omitted from his 1921 Nobel Prize, remained invisible and unacknowledged throughout. But the comparison itself is simple—perhaps too simple to be properly understood. In Einstein's case the variable is the observer, who cannot be certain of their location or velocity in space-time without reference to their coordinate system (varying as it might from one observer to another). In Heisenberg's case the variable is the particle, whose precise location and velocity cannot be determined at one and the same time by a single observer. By the rules of the double comparison, then, Einstein's subject (the observer) is to Heisenberg's object (the particle) as Einstein's objective (determining one's own location and velocity) is to Heisenberg's all too subjective coordinate system.

What we need at this point is a physical equivalent of the double negative. And we find it in the concept of the black hole: the self-differentiating variable of spatial extension divided from within by the singularity of gravity attracting gravity—the so-called "event horizon" of a space disappearing into time. Though we have no very good idea of what actually happens in the interior of a black hole (how could we, in the absence of event?), it is clear that contraction plays a major role in it. Thus if the positive value of c gives us evidence of an expanding universe, its negative counterpart, if only by analogy, would give us a graphic example of what a universal contraction would be like. (All metaphors are black holes, but not all black holes are metaphors.)

Why compare black holes and metaphors at all? Put in the simplest terms, the event horizon of a black hole is a subject/object shift, a mutual inversion, or figure–ground reversal, of eventual ends and means. If an event occurs in the form of a unit space divided by unit time, then its counterpart on the other side of the event horizon would be an inversion of this, the nonevent of unit time divided by unit space. I am speaking in metaphors, of course, since such an anomaly is beyond the range of empirical observation. Fine, but if the event horizon is only a metaphor, of what is it a metaphor?

Experts distinguish two basic components of the metaphor: the tenor, the subject, or venue, or designated element, and the vehicle, its agency, objective, or means of transformation. In that sense space, or extension, is the tenor of an event, and time is the vehicle, or agentive. But this still does not account for the event horizon, or what takes place there.

For a true subject/object shift, or reciprocity of perspectives, corresponds directly to a double-proportional comparison—the metaphor *of* a metaphor, or what I have elsewhere termed "the second power of trope" (Wagner 1986), and must do so to qualify for a complete subject/object shift, or transposition of ends and mean (trope and vehicle). *Metaphor × metaphor = double-proportional comparative = subject/object shift = complete transposition of ends and means.* This is the only thing that could possibly *unhappen* at the event horizon of a black hole.

If you do not have a convenient black hole to practice on, you can try this simple experiment in double-proportional inversion with the more easily obtained electric motor-generator instead. Possibly the most ubiquitous agentive in the modern technological arsenal, it is the energy-converter that makes a wheel of the magnet and a magnet of the wheel, deploying the same basic mechanical advantage for both the use and the generation of electric current. In the simplest terms, you mount a spinning coil of wire, called an armature, within a fixed and slightly larger coil, called a stator coil, so that the resulting inversion can be effective in one of two ways: (1) if electric current is run through the coils, a self-reactive electromagnetic field is induced between them, and a physical twisting motion, or torque, is produced; (2) if, on the other hand, an artificial torque from some outside source is introduced into the system, the result is the generation of an electric current. Expressed as a double proportion, then: torque is to current as current is to torque—two physical effects used twice and in reverse order the second time.

The copresence of the tactic of self-reflexive duality in both the black hole and the electric motor-generator raises the intriguing question of whether the phenomenon as a whole is of human design, and merely projected upon the natural world, or whether it is inherent in the physical nature of things. Is the double-comparative, subject/object shift, reciprocity of perspectives, or whatever one wishes to call it, explained by the innate phenomenal nature of things, or is it merely a projection of the quality and character of human cognition?

In what way can the event-horizon phenomenality of the black hole be understood as a counterpart of the event-producing action of the electrical motor–generator complex? How is energy, and more specifically gravitic energy, related to the happening of things? Is it possible that the Newtonian dogmas of classical physical mechanics have gotten the nature of gravity wrong?

Understood in human (anthropological) terms rather than rationalistic ones, the thing we have so confidently objectified as "gravity" is a "spin-off," so to speak, of the failure of our physics to deal effectively with motion. For the record: gravity is not a *force* (as in "forces of nature") but an *effect* (as in "side-effect"). To be more specific, it is a *countereffect* (like an "equal but opposite reaction") or figure–ground reversal, of *angular momentum*, or *spin*. A gyroscope, for example, enhances its own inertia by accelerating its spin.

Originally discovered by the Nobel laureate Richard Feynman, the provable fact that gravitic attraction is not a direct function of mass has been suppressed or ignored by the experts on physical mechanics. Possibly this is because the relation between inertia and gravity, which Einstein insisted are one and the same thing, has been generally omitted from consideration. The proof of the pudding is in the gyroscope: just as a spinning gyroscope enhances its own moment of inertia (the "steadying" effect, often used to steady ships at sea) by concentrating its mass at the periphery of its spin, and thereby inverting centrifugal force to produce a *centripetal* effect, so any massive object suspended in space—a planet, star, or even a whole galaxy—will achieve the same effect by revolving on its axis, and in that sense manufacturing its own gravity, converting its angular momentum into gyroscopic stability.

Not unsurprisingly, this counterintuitive understanding of gravity is likewise a consequence of the double-proportional comparison: in this case centripetal force is to centrifugal force as inertia is to gravity. In this way the anomaly originally noted by the astronomer Fritz Zwicky and later confirmed by the careful researches of Vera Rubin, that the mass of a rotating galaxy is insufficient to provide the gravitic attraction necessary to hold it together, conceals an astounding refutation of the classic Newtonian identification of mass with gravity. From this we can draw the conclusion that the black hole at the center of the galaxy is both the product and the producer of the galaxy itself, and that its incumbent event horizon encompasses the obviation of the galaxy as an event.

This brings us to the dicey question of whether or not the event horizon can "happen" to itself, become, so to speak, its own event, or in other words whether it has an ontological status or not. As Bertrand Russell, an expert on paradoxes of this sort, might remind us, if it could "happen to itself," it would not be a horizon, for half of it would then be on the other side of its own horizon, and if it could not happen to itself, then it would not be an event. What this tells us is that it is a specifically ontological chiasmus, a determiner of paradoxes, and belongs to the same logical family as Gödel's Proof ("using logic, this [very] hypothesis cannot be proven to be true," and of course, by that very same logic, cannot be proven false, either). Immersed in this conundrum, it is easy to lose sight of the fact that the double-proportional comparison is the logical basis of analogy itself, meaning that a chiasmus cannot be an analogy of itself.

So we return to the question, posed earlier, of whether the double-proportional comparison, in any of its many transformations and disguises, is a function of the inherent nature of reality, or merely a project of our own cognitive apparatus. It is a very difficult question to answer; not only do self-reflexive dualities (two words used twice and in reverse order the second time) define the logical space of Freud's subconscious, they also form the paradigmatic basis for Lévi-Strauss's Canonic Formula for Myth.

Known more broadly as the self-definitive syntax of the aphorism (Karl Kraus: "an aphorism is either half true or one and a half times true"), the format itself has been objectified by many peoples around the world as the archetypal form of auto-verificational rhetoric—the art, so to speak, of telling more than the truth. Thus when I asked my Daribi confreres in Papua New Guinea, "What makes a man a big man; is it having more wives and pigs than others?" they replied, "If a man can talk *porigi* well, he gets all the wives and pigs he needs."

Perhaps the most influential rhetorical incorporation of perspectival reciprocity was recovered by Tania Stolze Lima (1999) from the Yudjá (Juruna) indigenes of eastern Brazil: "When a pig looks at a pig, it sees a human being, but when it looks at a human being it sees another pig." A classic instance of chiasmatic figure–ground reversal, this elegant allusion to the perceptual subject/object shift has nothing whatever to do with how pigs perceive things or what they actually do perceive, but subserves its whole function as sucker bait for the literal minded. An elaborate double comparison of self-similarity disguised as the other and other-similarity disguised as the self, it blithely transposes the form and the content of the message with one another, turns the manner of saying it into the message itself.

For the Daribi, this agency devolves upon a form of political power-speech called "*porigis*," an agglutinized combination of *po* ("speech," "language," "information") + *-r-* (ligative marker) + *igi* (agentive infix for "action intended elsewhere") = *po-r-igi*, literally "the speech of remote intentions." This deserves some comment, for it serves as a derivative of a paradigm of what could be called "lapsed intention participles" that demonstrate the remote-intentional world space of Daribi imagination. Thus *-igi-* is one of two markers for intentional deictics: *-aga* for proximal intention and *-igi-* for distal, or remote, intention. Examples: *ena tuagazare*, "I came here to eat," and *ena tugi-pobau*, "I am going there to eat." The lapsed intentions come into play when completive forms indicating the results of the intended actions are added in sequence. These come in three forms: *-sogo-*, indicating successful completion of intended action; *-digi-*, indicating unsuccessful completion; and *-guri-*, indicating "almost but not quite" completed action. Example: *ena tugi guri dai*, "I went to eat, almost succeeded in eating but not quite, and here I am."

Is it possible to incorporate a subject/object shift within ordinary speech patterning? The Daribi continuative verb *begerama* means literally "turning back on itself," thus Daribi define the effect of *porigi* in their own language as *po begerama pusabo po*, literally "the talk that turns back on itself as it is spoken."

What does this really mean? Perhaps the best evidence for the self-transformative character of the reciprocity of perspectives lies in its effect on language itself, which ceases to be an instrument of communication and takes on the role of communicator or persuader—that of the user rather than the tool. Like a form of paraverbal karate, it transects the boundary that it itself has made, making the means its end and its end the means themselves.

But what is intended by "ends" and "means" in this context? We have no direct evidence that the thing we call "energy" exists at all, except in the point-event that transforms one "kind" of energy into another, as the optic nerve transforms the light from a star into the neuronic energy of the central nervous system. But that ambiguity only goes to show that there is no such thing as photonic energy or neuronic energy, but only the liminality of the point-event that transforms the one "kind" of effect into the other. When taken out of context and understood as an agentive factor in its own right, this conflation of ambiguity and limitlessness defines what Victor Turner called "liminality" (from the Latin *limen*, meaning boundary or limit). Though normally invisible and undetectable, like energy or, for that matter, metaphor, liminality can only be inferred, and not witnessed directly. In other words (and what is a metaphor but "other words"?), metaphor, liminality, and energy share the same description, and since "things equal to the same thing are likewise equal to each other," they might as well be the same thing.

Hence the essence of what Turner, to the dismay of his colleagues, called "antistructure" sums up the liminal contiguity of the thing I am talking about here, that which is neither itself nor some other thing, the event horizon of the phenomenal. That much is evident from his brilliant exegesis of ritual in *Revelation and divination in Ndembu ritual* as "expressing what cannot be thought of, in view of thought's subjugation to essences" (1975: 187). Ritual is the antistructure of "metaphor spread out" and its liminality, the ubiquitous event horizon projected by obviation. It is the end result of a self-modeling dialectic, one that, to paraphrase Victor Zuckerkandl, "grows in a dimension perpendicular to time" (1973: 191).

Self-modeling, like Turner's concept of liminality, is based on a mutual inversion of subject and object, ends and means, between the respective researcher and their indigenous confreres, in which each party assumes the motivating perspectives of the other, and adopts it as the basis of their understanding of that other. Drawing initially from Freud's notion of "the transference" in psychoanalysis, in which patient and analyst adopt each other's strategy in effecting a resolution, and dubbed "reverse anthropology" (Wagner 1981; Kirsch 2006), it was applied across the board in the 1960s by key figures in the discipline like Turner himself, David M. Schneider, Claude Lévi-Strauss, Carlos Castaneda, and Clifford Geertz, turning "social anthropology" into "cultural anthroplogy," and setting the stage for the "postmodernist" critiques that followed. At a single stroke a formerly digital (e.g., concerned with categories and classifications) approach gave way to an analogic one (concerned with self and other modeling, representation, and perspectival reciprocities).

This raises the question of whether the medium of representation itself, the extensional basis of space and time, is a self-modeling phenomenon. Both space and time are forms of extension, but they "extend" in very different ways, so different that temporal extension is practically invisible and depends exclusively on its more obvious and tangible spatial counterpart for any kind of recognition or understanding. At a guess, one might suggest that the two forms of extension are completely opposite to one another, that space extends the world and time intends the moment. But even that sounds like an oversimplification, like the puerile "spacetime" concept proposed by Einstein and Minkowski, which simply identifies the two forms of extension with one another, in spite of the more than obvious differences between them.

It should be clear, then, that we are dealing with two very different sorts of variables here, those of space and time, on one hand, and those of difference and similarity, on the other, and that the only logical form in which the two can coexist is that of the chiasmus or double-proportional comparison: *time is the difference between itself and space; space is the similarity between them.*

By this criterion Einstein had a lot to answer for when he hypothesized the "four-dimensional spacetime continuum," for he fell victim to the subject/object shift or unconscious transposition of ends and means. He mistook the four necessary terms of the double-proportional comparison for dimensions, and redefined the two different forms of extension as "coordinate systems."

But it was the Meso-American civilizations, not those of the Old World, who integrated chiasmatic logic completely within their ontology. It is a well-known fact that we do not perceive things at the moment they actually happen; there is always a brief time-lapse or "reaction time" between the actual happening of an event and the moment we really become aware of it. We gaze always into a recollected past. This is because it takes our cognitive apparatus a certain amount of time to assemble the raw data of perception and turn it into a thing we can recognize from our memory. So the question arises of how to objectify the perceptual time-lapse within the very recording of time, to involve temporal reaction time—the very medium of recollection—within the predictive anticipation of events. The trick would be to record each objectified time-unit (like hour, day, month, year) twice in computing the result: once for the lapse between itself and the previous unit, and once again for the lapse between itself and the next one. This double action makes the awareness of time and its passing one and the same thing. I shall use the ancient Mayan Long Count Calendar as an example, for the "second attention" chiasmatic action is made obvious in its workings.

This is not a circular movement, despite what we may think; time is not a wheel, and our circular devices are less than helpful in tracking its ostensible motion. The ancient Mayans turned the corner on time reckoning. The technique is baby-simple, and it goes like this: perceptual reaction time works at right angles to the actual, invisible happening of events—you represent the one (either one) by a vertical bar, and the other by a horizontal one. Then the objectified event, like a date on the Mayan calendar, is represented as the point of interaction of the two bars. It is an involution of the two measures, the one representing cognitive reaction time, and the other representing the out-of-awareness happening being tracked.

The net result of this ingenious form of representation is that it makes the two kinds of temporal interval—the subjective or internal, and the objective or external—substitutable for one another, like the two sides of an equation. Either can be represented as vertical or horizontal, provided that the other is the opposite (see diagram, below). Time and our perception of time are the two constants; how they combine with one another is the variable.

Study the accompanying diagram carefully. The Mayans never recorded the entire cycles or time periods directly: the only thing they recorded was a five-place numerical day sign on their monuments, signifying when auspicious, memorable events had occurred, or would occur. These represented the five intersection points of the six named, objectified time periods that make up the Long Count Calendar. They were intercalated by fractal, internal self-division, or what might be called "binary involution." The Long Count itself consisted of thirteen *Baktuns*, so the first number recorded which *Baktun* of the thirteen was present on that day. There are twenty *Katuns* in a *Baktun*, and so the second number records which *Katun* of the current *Baktun* that day represents. There are eighteen *Tuns* in a *Katun*, and the third number records which of those *Tuns* it is. There are twenty *Uinal* in a *Tun*, and the fourth number tells you which *Uinal* is current on that day, just as the fifth number represents which of the twenty *Kin*, or individual days, it is today.

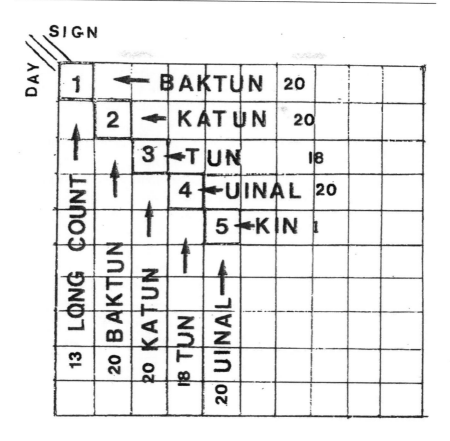

Binary involution in the Mayan Long Count. "The challenge in Mayan chronotopics lies in understanding that time exists only in the intersections of the cycles, and not otherwise in the cycles themselves."

What we have here is not simply an overelaborate form of the reciprocity of perspectives, but rather the extensional or expandable format of the subject/object shift, or double-proportional comparison. The effect is that of a catenary series of double-proportional comparisons, each comparing itself to and being compared with the previous and subsequent time periods. It is a second-attention representation of temporal stasis and duration, drawn to the exact scale of our perception of time, and in that way unique in our experience of temporal representations.

By comparing itself twice, once with the larger cycle that contains it, each cycle can be identified with a function that is totally unfamiliar to our mathematics, that of the self-determining variable, a function that compares itself to other things as it compares to itself (viz. "time is the *difference* between itself and space . . . space is the similarity between the two" [Wagner 2001: xv]). The concept of a double-proportional duality, a form of two-ness that operationally compares itself with itself in exactly the same way as it compares to other things, is distributed widely in Papua New Guinea. Gregory Bateson, who called it schismogenesis, found it as a major organizing principle among the Iatmul people of the Sepik River. The Daribi people of Mt. Karimui introduced it to me as *sidari-si* (literally "the two-together two"), and claim it is the pivotal or most important number in their mathematics. Working on a sudden hunch, I asked my confreres whether it has something to do with balance. "Ah yes," they said, "we call that thing *usu si si* ['sufficient two-two's'] or *si usu si* ['two sufficient two'];" and added, "that's so you can go straight."

Keeping in mind that what we are dealing with here is implicitly a mutual inversion of ends and means, or subject and object, the concept can easily be misunderstood as some form of overrationalized reciprocity on the material or social scale, as in Mauss's *Essai sur le don* (reciprocity without the perspectives), or, inversely, some form of idealized cultural patterning (perspective without the reciprocity), when its basic chiasmatic nature is ignored or misinterpreted.

Actually, it was Bateson, while searching for a modern-world analogue of the indigenous Melanesian concept of schismogenesis, who discovered it in the modern technological principle of automation. In fact his argument has a close parallel with the ontology of self-regulating devices, beginning with the early modern governor mechanism on a steam engine, and leading eventually to the cybernetic feedback loop, with its global reach and significance. The mechanical and electronic expression of the principle I have been examining here has engineered an invisible transposition of ends and means between human users and artifactual used, a shift between subject and object that has rather vaguely been recognized as an "industrial revolution."

Just what might this mean in logical terms? As Bateson put it in the 1958 epilogue to his monograph *Naven*: "The ideas themselves are extremely simple, all that is required is that we ask not about the characteristics of a system in which the chains of cause and effect are lineal, but about the characteristics of systems in which the chain of cause and effect is circular, or more than circular" (1958: 188). We explain the way things happen, and therefore remember them, in a cause-and-effect sequence—first the cause, then the effect. Applying the model of cause and effect to anything, including thought itself, is what we mean by logic or reason, as in "it is only rational to assume that the cause comes first, and the effect comes afterward." The problem with this "easy answer" is that it mystifies the relation between the thing we are calling "cause" and the thing we call "effect" by (a) pretending they are two different things, and (b) pretending that the "relation" between them is simply a temporal one of "before" and "after." In fact, the ingrained habit of thinking like that disguises a simple little trick, and that trick is the fact that (a) the event we are talking about could not happen at all if the cause and the effect were not one and the same thing, and (b) we must insert an imaginary space or interval between the two alleged "things" in order to believe that one of them "causes" or "acts upon" the other. "Cause" and "effect" are only arbitrary distinctions, results of thinking about things in a certain way.

The proof of this is that the "causal" relation can be turned around—that is, reversed or inverted—and still make the same kind of sense, though in a "funny" rather than a "serious" way. In a joke, for instance, you get the "effect" first, as the opening scenario or "setup" of the joke, and afterward you are surprised by the "cause," or "punchline," because it is (a) not the one you were expecting and (b) not where you expected it be (i.e., after the thing it is supposed to explain). Thus a joke belongs to one of those "systems" whose chains of cause and effect are those that Bateson would consider "circular" or "more than circular."

From this evidence it can easily be observed that an expression that contained both the "serious" or agentive articulation of causality and its "humorous" inversion would constitute in and of itself a double-proportional comparison of the two logical types, in that it would describe a compound analogy that was analogous to itself in two distinctly different (in fact opposite) ways—what we could call a self-analogy. In terms of the discussion to date, it would not only "stand for itself," but also integrate all of the properties of the reciprocity of perspectives included thus far: the figure–ground reversal, subject/object shift, transposition of ends and means, cybernetic feedback loop, etc. In other words, the self-analogic form is commutative throughout the range of its possible permutations and combinations. Curiously, however, this is not simply a matter of self-similarity, as the fractal mathematicians ("chaos scientists") would have it, for it is self-differentiating as well, and contains both features within the same analogic construct.

What do humor, science, religion, and shamanic power practices have in common? Each in its own way is an "overmystification," if that term be allowed, of the chiasmatic signature pattern that transforms the purport and intent of an idea into the means or tactics by which it was conceptualized or imagined in the first place. The secret of what could be called "the logic of invention" is no more mysterious and no less counterintuitive than the nature of time itself. Yet another permutation of the double-proportional comparison or transposition of ends and means, it echoes Aristotle's understanding of mimesis, or imitative learning: invention is the difference between itself and reality; reality is the similarity between the two. Just as invention or imitation is the means of reality (realization), so the only reality is that of invention itself.

What does it mean to "invent" reality? Let me cite the works of Carlos Castaneda as an example. The Peruvian-American anthropologist Carlos Arana Castaneda is often accused of inventing the teachings of don Juan, as well as their protagonist and his convenors, and that may well have been the case. Even if we grant that possibility, the question of what "invention" may mean in that context takes precedence, if only because all such accounts are "inventions" in one form or another. Did Carlos invent himself by inventing don Juan, or was it really some anonymous Mexican nicknamed "Juan" invented himself by means of Carlos? Which of them is the end, and which the means, of the other? Without further information (not provided), the question is impossible to answer, and reminds one of the old joke: "Were the *Iliad* and the *Odyssey* written by the Homer we know, or by some other Greek of the same name?"

The fact remains that the real inventor was the chiasmatic power relation, the authorial transposition of ends and means, without which there would have been no dialogue, and no books. Each of the Castaneda books is about the way it was written, in this sense. A good example of this is the discussion of humor and "seeing" in Castaneda's *A separate reality* (1971), a ploy by which don Juan hopes to introduce Carlos to "the second attention," a level of consciousness based on perceiving things through the reciprocity of perspectives rather than merely looking at it directly. The best example of this is the "humoring" (e.g., patronizing) of ordinary perception ("you look as you think, and think as you look") by interposing the "funny edge of things"—that is, the incongruity produced by transposing the roles of cause and effect in a humorous situation, and so enabling the "seeing" of nonlinear causality.

Most significantly, the office of explanation itself is understood and presented in chiasmatic terms in the book *Tales of power* (1975), where it is called "the sorcerer's explanation." In terms of the present discussion, this involves putting self-differentiating factors in the double proportion, like time, invention, and what don Juan calls the energy body (*chi*), in context as examples of the *nagual*, or second attention, and their passive, first-attention counterparts, such as language ("the Inventory") and cultural convention in general, as examples of the *tonal*. Hence the sorcerer's explanation, or "True Pair," as don Juan calls it, scans as yet another permutation of the chiasmatic double comparison: *nagual* is the difference between itself and the *tonal*; *tonal* is the similarity between the two.

The parallel with indigenous highland Mexican ontology is so close that there can be no doubt as to who invented invention in the first place. According to Miguel León-Portilla (1963), it was Moyocoyani, "the god that invented itself" (derived from the reflexive form of the Nahuatl verb *yucoyo*, meaning "to invent, or conceive mentally"). Castaneda's self-invention, one might say, comes from a very old and proud tradition.

This does not mean, of course, that Carlos's grasp of the second attention was infallible: for instance, he missed the point of the memory exercise ("exorcism" would be a better term) that don Juan calls "The Recapitulation," and considers a vital step in the training of a warrior, perhaps the most essential one of all. Presented as a kind of life-review, reexperiencing all the significant events in one's life "in the way they really happened and not as you remember them," its real purpose or hidden agenda is to reconstitute the concept of "memory" itself on a nonlinear basis, reliving it in second-attention ("heightened awareness") terms. In this respect it corresponds exactly to the "enlightenment" achieved by the Buddha after a similar life-review under the Bodhi tree.

In the Mexican version, the warrior must spend weeks, months, or even years confined in a crate, cave, or similarly enclosed area with an outline of the significant events of their life as a mnemonic prompt, recalling each event exactly as it had occurred at the time, while carefully punctuating the exchange of energies with an intake and expulsion of breath (note the resemblance to prana Yoga). The purpose of the memory-review, however, is not simply a more veridical redaction of the sequence of events in one's life, but, as the exchange of energies might suggest, a complete transformation (e.g., transposition of ends and means) of the concept of memory itself into a second attention venue, converting both memory and its recollected content from a linear or sequential format to a nonlinear one. Basically, the technique uses our commonplace understanding of memory as a distraction, so that the subject will undergo a transition into second attention without being aware of it.

The real secret lies in the use of the double-proportional comparison to mediate the relation between past and present, in a technique not dissimilar to the one reviewed earlier in the case of the Mayan calendar: memory has nothing to do with the past; its only purpose is to rearrange (predict) the future. Understood in this way, the Meso-American Recapitulation, like the Buddha's enlightening experience under the Bodhi tree, served to detach the subject from their self-imposed subservience to past events and experience, and allow them to experience the present moment as it truly is—as something that is about to happen.

The memory, as it were, models itself upon itself. But at this point the reader is entitled to ask just what, exactly, does self-modeling mean? When don Juan criticized first-attention logic, he did so in second-attention terms, using the double-proportional comparison: "You look as you think and you think as you look," meaning that thought models perception ("looking") and perception thought so precisely that the combination models our whole experience of the world. Though each, when taken by itself, affords a fairly limited understanding, their mutual modeling provides an intimation of how conscious awareness might have come about in the first place. As a diagnostic feature of the second attention, self-modeling makes subject and object, or ends and means, into conjoint parts of a single, self-contained understanding. Like time, and like invention, it is a self-differentiating variable: self-modeling is the difference between itself and mimesis; mimesis is the similarity between the two.

CHAPTER 2

Facts picture us to themselves
Wittgenstein's propositions

"Facts picture us to themselves" is the chiasmatic inversion of Ludwig Wittgenstein's most distinctive proposition, "We picture facts to ourselves." The key word here is "picture," for it means we think in images, not words, know and understand things according to the pictures our minds make of them. These are called "heuristics" when used in a deliberate pedagogical way, and may have nothing else to do with the "fact" they are helping us to understand. If you turn this around, make the appropriate subject/object shift—facts picture us to themselves—you will get a sort of undeveloped negative of yourself in the fact of the fact that is trying to understand exactly how you are trying to understand it. In other words, heuristics are retroactive; we ourselves are understood in our understanding of the facts.

Wittgenstein was born into a world afflicted by a deadly but invisible neurosis, a need to explain gone viral. To an outside observer it would appear as an innate compulsion to find utilitarian rationalizations that explain the "workings" of things. As the neurosis took hold, from the industrial revolution onward, it began to dominate all fields of human endeavor and all aspects of society, not only the political and the social, but even the frontiers of research and production: things (and people) "worked" because they fit the habit structure of the population, and they fit the habit structure of the population because they worked. Catch-22: double-proportional comparison/double-comparative proportionalism.

In commonplace on-the-street jargon, the "fact of the fact that is trying to understand exactly how you are trying to understand it" is called automation ("it works by itself"), meaning roughly "it works by itself as a purely mechanical approximation of human spontaneity." (One of my best friends in graduate school was working on a computer program to incorporate the factor of originality in musical composition.) If the literal meaning of "automation" is "a device that works by itself," then Wittgenstein might fairly be accused of originating, in the *Tractatus logico-philosophicus* (1961), an epistemology that deduces itself from itself, or causes itself to cause itself to come into being as such.

Unable to recognize the nonlinear logic by which the successive propositions of the *Tractatus* displace, augment, or negate (obviate) one another, Wittgenstein is obliged to perceive the whole text as a kind of Gödel's Proof or Russell's Paradox of self-contradictory epistemology—a set of conclusions that is both right and wrong at the same time. He affirms its viewpoint only to retract it, and retracts it only to reaffirm it again. What he fails to "get," as it were, is that the whole corpus of argument is a profound statement about the role of analogy in furthering discursive continuity, that analogy is by its very nature nonlinear, and that its very nonlinearity often takes precedence over linear logic, that any analogy involved in the perception of reality is at the same time a reality of the perception of analogy.

Hence the illusion of meaninglessness in the *Tractatus*, what Wittgenstein calls its "nonsensical" quality, is a direct and deliberate outcome of its being written in double-proportional comparatives. This gives an unusual piquancy to the individual propositions themselves—they are self-contained and self-isolating, each creates its own contextual ambience, a climate of thought that is both reflected and refracted in the others, often by implication only. The very fact that they both undercut and support each other, that their logical precedence is neither ordered nor chaotic, gives a good indication of why Wittgenstein found it necessary to impose an overly precise decimal indexing system upon them. One counts best when one does not know what one is counting.

Wittgenstein's philosophy can be seen to answer the question "What difference would it make to epistemology if meaning were coded in images rather than words?" Linguistic images, for someone of Wittgenstein's musical upbringing, are primarily acoustical—sound images like the themes of a symphony, rather than visual ones. This calls for a very different form of syntax than we find in most linguistic studies. A proposition, in Wittgenstein's sense, is an internalized echo, an echo from within the ambience of lexical referentiality, rather than from the outside. In these terms human intentionality might be most profitably compared to the manner in which a bat finds its way in the dark. Just as the bat utters short, sharp, meaningless cries to echolocate its way around obstacles in the dark, so the darkness itself defines the source of those cries as the very position and existence of the bat. But, you object, by the time the bat receives its echo, it is already in a different place than the one the darkness had defined for it, and it must utter yet another cry to keep with its ongoing motion. Hence the subject/object shift: the subjective bat (where it thinks it is) and the objective bat (where the surrounding darkness knows it to be) are always in two different places that seem to be one. And they differ from one another by the span of intent.

In effect the bat is always getting ahead of itself without knowing how or why: the bat flies under its own radar, never hears the echo of its intent. In this respect there is a very big difference between bats and human beings: the bat uses its voice in a very exact but meaningless way—it simply utters syllables to echolocate its way through the darkness around it. But the human being does the very opposite of that, something inside-out and turned around: it pretends a meaning into the syllables it utters so as to echolocate the presence of something dark within it. The cries it utters—sound-coded points of memory reference called "words"—are just as meaningless (because arbitrary) as those of the bat, but the echoes it gets back from that something dark within it are the very essence of meaningful intent, and are called metaphors.

A metaphor is one word's way of understanding another, in a way that is kept as a secret from both of them.

Even if the bat had perfect eyesight and flew only in the daylight, it would still have to pretend a mysterious darkness around itself so that the trick of echolocation would work properly. Even if the human being had perfect insight and knew that the darkness inside of itself were pure light, it would still have to pretend a profound darkness within so that its pretense of meaningfulness would win the acceptance of its peers. Otherwise its knowledge of itself would give the lie to its claims of being human. For by the time the human being learns that meaningfulness is only a pretended quality, a necessary foil to protect the credibility of social communication, it is already in a different place than it was before, and has learned to communicate by remote intentions.

Consciousness is what happens when meaning draws pictures of itself, using you yourself—both the subject and the object of the pictures—as its agency in doing so, in the way that the one you see in the mirror allows you to see itself seeing itself. Wittgenstein's propositions make artificiality the supreme test of veracity; without human intervention nothing would be believably real. Facts picture us to themselves in the way that the artist Jan Vermeer used a camera obscura to reverse the reciprocity of perspectives on itself, thereby reprojecting the otherwise distant vanishing point into the viewer—a kind of soul-capture—or as the zero sign used in mathematics objectifies a particular quality of somethingness in order to signify the nothingness that it really means. There is no reality without the perception of reality, and no perception without the objectification of reality as such. Did Wittgenstein bare his soul to the world in writing the *Tractatus*, or did the world bare its soul to him?

Commentary on the propositions

2.033   *Form is the possibility of structure.*

Comment: A symphony does not have a form; it reaches for one. In other words, one could as well say that it is precisely those ways that a given symphony does not accord with the generic form of "a symphony" that makes it a real symphony, as, say, that its accordance with the generic form makes it a symphony. We know of no symphony that does not fall somewhere between these two extremes, nor would I want to hear one. Even a word or sign that was either completely ambiguous or one that was completely unambiguous would be useless for purposes of its own self-expression.

2.1   *We picture facts to ourselves.*

Comment: The fact of the picture is the picture of the fact. We are the fact or act of picturing facts to ourselves—our own picture to others and their own picture to ourselves. We have no other self; self or soul is how I have been pictured by others, and how I have pictured others to myself. Outside of this discourse, and inside of it as well, there are no human beings, only bodily functions and our apprehensions about them.

               So, you begin to get the picture. Unfortunately, at the same moment, the picture begins to get you. We do not know or state (describe) the substances or contents of things or even actions in the world except to agree or disagree about the boundary conditions for perception. This means that we simply lay ourselves open to the ways in which these "contents" themselves participate in our acknowledgment of them. We merely create the frames; the pictures themselves create our framing of them. The world as we know it is an entirely ergative creation, in which the active and the passive exchange roles, and in the act of exchanging roles account for the phenomenon that we call "perception."

Hence the chiasmatic corollary to Proposition 2.1, "Facts picture us to themselves," is much stronger than the original. It is the facts, after all, of our constitution, as individuals or groups, that take the major role in picturing us, to ourselves, or to the universe around us.

2.172   *A picture cannot, however, depict its pictorial form: it displays it.*

Comment: A picture does not have hands, does not have eyes; does not have agency, so that a picture, like a mirror, borrows our agency to bring about the things we choose to see in it. A picture incorporates the viewer as the necessary (incorporative) part of viewing it, and thus "makes" the viewer incorporate it.

This may in fact sound trivial, but a moment's reflection will show that it is exactly what a mirror does. To depict itself, a picture would have to incorporate a miniaturized version of its totality as one of its parts or aspects (and thus do itself to itself) and thus acquire the property of self-scaling (holography or nonlocality). When this does happen, as in the case of a 3-D hologram, the picture displays itself as the boundary condition of its own objectification, or separation off from the world around it. In this same sense, a language cannot merge with the world of its saying without ceasing to be a language, nor can a creator-god emerge from the self-scaling necessity of creation and still claim sovereignty of being. A mother lives on in her daughter's embryo.

The next two propositions follow from the point of this.

2.173   *A picture represents its subject from a position outside it. (Its standpoint is its representational form.) That is why a picture represents its subject correctly or incorrectly.*

2.174   *A picture cannot, however, place itself outside its representational form.*

Comment: It cannot, for this very reason, depict itself, nor depict itself depicting it-self, nor even depict others depicting it, for each of these would require a separate standpoint. This is the essential irony of what is called a sense of humor, for a joke is always about how its initial scenario got there in the first place, but then had to be explained (or unexplained) in the second place. The artist Jan Vermeer tried to paint a picture (*The art of painting*) of a picture depicting itself, and failed so brilliantly that he actually succeeded (most other artists succeed so brilliantly that they actually fail). To put the matter very diffidently, but also correctly: all jokes are on time.

There is a very basic, and necessary, connection between the evolution of human sentience and the ability to "get the point of" or deal with humor. In a certain fundamental sense, because all humor is about pictures, all pictures are about humor, or at least about the humor of self-depiction. We may take a cosmic example as the best instance of this. Under any conceivable circumstances, and regardless of the means or methods by which the picture was obtained, our notion of the cosmic surround is at best only a picture, that is, a picture from a certain standpoint. Following the researches of Edwin Hubble, we have learned to interpret our depiction of the cosmos as one whose extensional properties are expanding. Though this is conventionally interpreted as the consequence of an apocryphal "big bang" origin of the universe, it has recently been observed (by another picture of the "picture") that the rate of cosmic expansion is not stable (as we would expect from a "big bang" explanation), but is itself accelerating. The significance of this (is it a better interpretation of "entropy," a sort of escape clause for the laws of thermodynamics?) depends on whether one accepts the subject depicted or the fact of depiction itself as the source of information about the cosmos. If Wittgenstein is correct, in other words, the idea of "dark energy" that cosmologists have invented to save their confidence in the "big bang" represents a mistake in judgment, interpreting the fact of depiction itself in terms of the subject depicted in it. It is like assuming that the picture we get of the universe is both a static picture and a moving parallax of that picture.

This leads directly to the next three propositions.

2.225   *There are no pictures that are true a priori.*

3   *A logical picture of facts is a thought.*

3.001   *"A state of affairs is thinkable": what this means is that we can picture it to*
               ourselves.

Comment: "But we have the empirical evidence for the background radiation of the
               big bang!"

               "Yeah you do, sure you do, and I have Halley's Comet in my
               basement."

               A picture is true to itself alone—any other depiction is incidental to
               its form. The results of the "big bang," or "background radiation of the
               big bang," constitute a single-frame description of the universe at a given
               time, a being thing. (Energy—as in $E = mc^2$—may be defined as that ef-
               fect that is not there anymore once you detect its traces; like a joke, see?)
               It is not a becoming thing: that is, it lacks the parallactic elevation of a
               humor that would see it in spite of its situation.

               To put it differently, that is, to make the necessary subject/object
               switch: we cannot sense ourselves—only others can do that. What we
               sense is only our moving point of view, which we assume to be part of the
               body that others tell us about. One does not see a point of view directly
               without losing it.

3.031   *It used to be said that God could create anything except what would be con-*
               trary to the laws of logic. The truth is that we could not say what an illogical
               world would look like.

Comment: So creation is not God's problem after all; it is ours.

               The need for a God may be defined simply and accurately as the need
               for a perspective different from any we could imagine. To understand
               that there is a kind of perfection that excludes entirely our knowing of it
               is to understand completely the holographic, or scale-retentive nonlocal-
               ity of the universe. The phenomenal world of the body—which always
               belongs to others—has been artificially superimposed on it.

               Wittgenstein's discourse up to this point, his discussion of pictures,
               facts, and thoughts (e.g., logic, *logos*, and the curious relation of God
               and creation to logic), has been dominated by a one-to-one correspond-
               ence between concept ("proposition") and the visual imagination (thus
               we have used the term "holography" advisedly). Henceforth we enter
               the realm of acoustics, the resonantial world of hominid communication,

and the music that was fundamental to Wittgenstein's apperception of the truth.

Music, like voice, is acoustic, and therefore tactile; it moves you, touches you, hits you in the gut. In contrast to the others, the great civilizations that developed from the so-called Indo-European, Finno-Ugric, and Semitic aggregates have provided the world with its great classical musics, its creator-gods that speak with a command voice.

3.141   *A proposition is not a blend of words (just as a theme in music is not a blend of notes).*
A proposition is articulate.

Comment: Music is not mosaic; mosaic is not music.

And a name, like a melody, a theme, or a rhythmical structure, is self-articulate. There is a fundamental difference here that has to do with the knowing of things in conjuncture with the saying of things.

One has to imagine the sentence to make a fact of the acoustical knowing of things. (The German term for a movement in a symphonic piece is *Satz*, a word that also means "sentence" in German.) What linguists call the lexicon is the world of imaginary sentences. Linguists call the structure-world of the real or imaginary sentence syntax, and most of Wittgenstein's propositional logic or philosophy from this point onward amounts to an effort to fix the parameters of syntactical reasoning into those of logical thought.

3.221   *Objects can only be named. Signs are their representatives. I can only speak about them: I cannot put them into words. Propositions can only say how things are, not what they are.*

Comment: At this point Wittgenstein is drawing ever closer to the nominalist philosophy taught at the University of Paris by Peter Abelard and others in opposition to the so-called realist philosophy of the Platonists, who insisted that names correspond to the real, true, or pure essences of things (objects), which exist somewhere in the universe in a pristine form. For the nominalists, the only thing one could know about something was its name, and the so-called essence was only a derivative of that fact.

3.26   *A name cannot be dissected any further by means of a definition; it is a primitive sign.*

Comment: Despite the well-known fact that the presumed one-to-one correspondence of "words to things" of the lexicon to the world of its reference or representation is haphazard and inexact, or perhaps because of that fact, there is no need to postulate an original ("primordial") formation of the lexicon (as, for instance, through the imitation of sounds in the names for things). What Wittgenstein is suggesting here is that the sound-correspondences that "name" things are interpolated from within any general set of acoustic signals (rather than derived from the referentials themselves), that the formation of the lexicon is inductive rather than deductive, and always in progress, that it is more like the process of storytelling than like that of reasoning.

An original lexicon is a legend in itself.

3.33   *In logical syntax the meaning of a sign should never play a role. It must be possible to establish logical syntax without mentioning the meaning of a sign; only the description of expression may be presupposed.*

Comment: In other words, every time we draw attention to the meaning or identity of a sign, word, or other linguistic element, every time we speculate in linguistic philosophy (in the way that Wittgenstein is doing here), we are entering the fairy-tale world of the putative original lexicon and its hypothetical formulation, and furthermore predicating the structural implications of syntax upon it. Language philosophy always works best when it can pretend to itself that the artifact language is a near-perfect copy of some inherent order that it seems to be expressing, or at least can be helped along by the attentions of the linguistic philosopher. But if most or all languages are far from perfect in that respect, or only "Platonic" in their reach for perfection, then attempts to redefine meaning, syntactic function, or propositional status in language, such as Wittgenstein scores Russell for, are not necessarily misguided. They are attempts to return to the legendary fairy-tale world of lexical formation and context determination regardless of whether that world existed or not.

Language, as Wittgenstein has envisioned it here, is a self-modeling subject, one that owes its (fabled) origin, complexity, and articulative power to its immediate use and usage, and so of course its general felicity in use and contemplation to this spontaneous origin. That is, anything we may know of language or do with language has nothing to do with the product ("artifact") language, except that it is coterminous with the innovations wrought upon it. We pretend that it has been there all the time, just as we do with our own intellect.

Its self-modeling capability is probably the most important thing we can know about language. Like Shakespeare's métier, Wittgenstein's "logic" proves nothing and disproves nothing, and yet when it is over one has the sinister feeling that everything worth saying has been said. (Prince Hamlet was extremely good at this: he acted himself mad to say the things no sane person would be allowed to utter on the public stage. Wittgenstein brought about the same effect by acting himself sane.) No wonder anthropology lacks a cover term for this kind of human activity; as a friend of mine once put it: "The anthropologist wants to be the figure as well as the ground."

This leads to what is probably the most candid of Wittgenstein's propositions about language.

4.002   *Man possesses the ability to construct languages capable of expressing every sense, without having any idea how each word has meaning or of what its meaning is—just as people speak without knowing how the individual sounds are produced.*

Everyday language is a part of the human organism and no less complicated than it.

It is not humanly possible to gather immediately from it what the logic of language is.

Language disguises thought. So much so, that from the outward form of the clothing it is impossible to infer the form of the thought beneath it, because the outward form of the clothing is not designed to reveal the form of the body, but for entirely different purposes.

The tacit conventions on which the understanding of ordinary language depends are enormously complicated.

Comment: Language is not inspired, nor is it structured, in such a way as to reveal its origins or purposes, or indeed anything else about the world in which it subsists, or that perhaps subsists in it. It is not about itself; better to say it is only about what to say next.

If language disguises thought, then thought itself, which must therefore occur in the form of language, likewise disguises language. (Language philosophy is one of its most preposterous disguises.) For the systole and diastole of breath, the most immediately vital of all the body's organic functions, not only serves as an internal metronome and capacitor for the iteration of language, but simultaneously serves for the rhythmic oxygenation and decarbonization of the blood and vital organs it subserves. Is the phenomenon of organic, carbon-based life therefore a sine qua non of the language phenomenon, at least in hominids? Of course it would have to be, and this is one of the ways in which thought disguises language, for without the precise articulation of the points and conclusions that have led us to it, in language, one could never discover that the elocution of language could be a matter of life and death. As it must have been, so many times, for our hominid ancestors. We breathe, essentially, through our vocal cords.

Put in the simplest terms, then, the fact that language disguises thought makes it possible both to utter a full disclaimer of our ability to understand or account for what language is, and to create logical paradoxes (Russell's Paradox, Epimenides's Paradox) that execute the same maneuver through the logical use of language itself. A trope or metaphor is the simplest way of using language to disguise thought (though a human being is a good try), yet without this device we would not be able to approximate meaning within the inventory function of language. As I have pointed out elsewhere (Wagner 2001), metaphor is language's way of figuring out what we mean by it. Note that, in order to make meaning a direct artifact of language usage in this way, I have had to execute a subject/object shift between the user of language and language itself as an agency in its own right. As the self-oxidizer and decarbonator of the speaking organism in this way, the breathing function of spoken language is the active agency, and the human ego or volitional self-construct the passive one. And if all our tropes or metaphors are in this sense instances of ergative usage, this makes the human ego, or articulative self-construct, into an ultimately passive, or acted-upon, agency. (Cf. Will Rogers: "Americans are lucky they don't get all the government they pay for.")

This makes the function of trope or metaphor, and therefore of course meaning itself, into that of a name, in the sense of Proposition 3.26 ("A name cannot be dissected any further by means of a definition; it is a primitive sign"). And hence our conclusions about that proposition about naming also apply in this case to those about meaning, to wit, that the formation of metaphor is inductive rather than deductive, that the sound-correspondences that "mean" things are interpolated from within any general set of acoustic signs, rather than derived from the referentials themselves. Meanings, like names, are applied from without.

The Daribi people, of Papua New Guinea, have a piece of folk wisdom about this, one that applies perfectly, as far as I can tell, to all instances of family life on all continents. It is that *a child is a wound from within.*

4.041   *There is a general rule by means of which the musician can obtain the symphony from the score, and which makes it possible to derive the symphony from the groove on the gramophone record, and, using the first rule, to derive the score again. That is what constitutes the inner similarity between these things which seem to be constructed in such entirely different ways. And that rule is the law of projection which projects the symphony into the language of musical notation. It is the rule for translating this language into the language of gramophone records.*

Comment: The concept of "inner similarities" and the law of projection are among the most intriguing generalities in Wittgenstein's work, if only because they allow for direct literal transliteration between the acoustic and the visual. Here, however, the symphony, as so often in Wittgenstein, comes to our rescue. It is not known how Beethoven, for instance, derived the symphony from the world, and his notebooks are of very little help. (Second-guessing great composers is always a kind of no-hope proposition.) Now, however, we have a little help from some forensic work done on a lock of Beethoven's hair almost two centuries after his death. From this evidence we learn that Beethoven had one hundred times as much lead in his body as the average Viennese citizen of his time (a result of drinking cheap wine, in which chunks of lead were used to settle out the impurities). The "inner similarities" come from the fact that both impotence and deafness are significant side-effects of acute lead poisoning. Ergo, by the law of projection, Beethoven derived his symphonies from the world by means of pure (Platonic) love.

4.015   *The possibility of all imagery, of all our pictorial modes of expression, is contained in the logic of depiction.*

Comment: We note that the *Tractatus* was written before the advent of Gregory
           Bateson's work, and the sharp distinction that Bateson drew between the
           digital and the analogic modes of communication and "information pro-
           cessing." In Batesonian terms, what this proposition seems to be saying is
           that we have at our disposal fully adequate means—which Wittgenstein
           calls "the law of projection" and "the logic of depiction"—for translating
           the digital into the analog and vice versa.

           In other words, the major point made in Proposition 4.002 regarding
           the function of language in disguising thought is at issue here too, for in
           this case phrases like "the law of projection" and "the logic of depiction"
           serve to disguise and hence underdetermine the distinction between the
           digital and the analogic. In the succeeding propositions Wittgenstein
           will refer to this mutually translative synthesis between the digital and
           the analogic as "sense." Sense occurs at the *limen*, or medial position
           of transition, between the digital and the analog, and is basically what
           Wittgenstein's notion of the logical proposition is all about.

4.016   *In order to understand the essential nature of a proposition, we should consider
           hieroglyphic script, which depicts the facts that it describes. And alphabetic
           script evolved out of it without losing what is essential to description.*

Comment: In other words the way in which language disguises thought in the case
           of a metaphor or analogy involves the fact that the digital expression of
           the metaphor confirms what its analogic aspect denies, and vice versa,
           and that this fundamental contradiction between expressive means and
           ends supplies the essential tension that turns meaning into sense. Rep-
           resentation or signification would be possible in a world without meta-
           phor; sense would not.

4.022   *A proposition shows its sense.*
           *A proposition shows how things stand if it is true. And it says that they do so
           stand.*

Comment: A proposition (or metaphor) acquires its agency or authority by perceiv-
           ing through two otherwise separate and distinct areas of experience; it

bridges them, and where there is no gulf (like that between the digital and analog), there is no bridge. It can be said or understood to perceive—that is, carry on the active role of perception in the way that a person does—because its use or agency carries the act of perception for the person, just as a bridge carries their movement. And if we could not carry forth the action of thinking or understanding with the use of proposition or metaphor, that must be because the metaphor thinks or understands for us.

4.026   *The meanings of simple signs (words) must be explained to us if we are to understand them.*
             With propositions, however, we make ourselves understood.

Comment: This is a good illustration of the difference between passive and active roles in the communication of knowledge, and of the role of ergative construction in the formation of a trope or proposition. To make oneself understood is to act upon oneself in such a way as to deflect one's condition into the passive mode, just as in an ergative construction, which charges or energizes the whole statement at the expense of its subject. Wittgenstein's "anthropology" is an anthropology of the subject.

             Had the *Tractatus* been composed in one of the Slavic or Finno-Ugric languages of Eastern Europe, wherein ergative usages predominate almost exclusively, propositions of this kind would have been superfluous, and the text would have been much shorter than it is now. As a bona fide Eastern European intellect, Wittgenstein faced the daunting task of introducing this mode of thinking and feeling to the minds of the Atlantic littoral. He was propositioning them. A symphony is likewise ergative, to the degree that the composer wishes themselves to be understood in it, because the composer had to suffer the victimage of its (inspirational) thematic material (e.g., how it suffered the ability to cope with it), before it could be conveyed to the audience in finished form. Hence the vast folklore on the suffering composer is more in the nature of a confessional than a fairy tale. (In the cases of convicts and also poets this is called "finishing the sentence.")

4.027   *It belongs to the essence of a proposition that it should be able to communicate a new sense to us.*

Comment: Since the conventional fabric of language is invariably composed of old or "tired" metaphors (cf. Lakoff and Johnson 1980), the innovative contrast of a proposition is that it communicates something new to the speaker.

4.03   *A proposition must use old expressions to communicate a new sense.*

     A proposition communicates a situation to us, and so it must be essentially connected with the situation.

     And the connection is precisely that it is its logical picture.

     A proposition states something only insofar as it is a picture.

Comment: So one might say that a memory, or act of remembering, must use the experiential traces of past events to make a picture of the past in the present—or is it the present in the past? It is precisely in the uncertainty or ambiguity between these two possibilities—past in the present and present in the past—that the subjectivity of memory exercises its charm. For our whole idea of temporal continuity depends upon a presentness that is subjected by the past—biography or history—whereas our whole idea of novelty and innovation (the invention of something that is totally new) depends upon a past that is subjected by the present.

     But the fact remains (or, in Wittgenstein's sense, the picture of the fact remains) that no matter which way the artifice of memory goes—past to present or present to past—the result takes the form of an ergative construction (*Geschichte als ob*/history as if); an emotion in the guise of "memory" has been repressed, and, like any other (ergative) subjugation of an ordinary or mundane state of affairs, it gains ten times the force of logic in its eventual expression (cf. the writings of Friedrich Nietzsche). Hence the fact that a proposition must subject itself internally in order to realize its status as a picture, or depiction of a state of affairs, turns the whole discussion of logic into a sense (emotion, feeling, as well as discursive disquisition on argumentation), and the whole disquisition on sense into something that resembles very closely Sigmund Freud's theory of repression. But what is a repression but a subjugation of the self? And what is a memory but another self?

     It is apparent in the *Tractatus* that Wittgenstein was very much aware of the foregoing, but that he chose to state the case in terms of propositions rather than memories or ergatives.

4.061   *It must not be overlooked that a proposition has a sense that is independent of*
             the facts: otherwise one can easily suppose that true and false are relations of
             equal status between signs and what they signify.

Comment: A proposition is an integral statement of its case; it is self-contained in
             terms of the logic that it alone articulates, which in that sense may be
             said to be self-modeled or self-modeling in terms of the statement of the
             proposition itself. A factual statement, on the other hand, is dependent
             on other statements, observations, empirical tests, opinions, biases, etc.
             This means that a proposition is subjected to itself by the forms of its
             iteration, whereas a factual statement is subjected to other matters that
             are not contained in it.

4.064   *Every proposition must already have a sense: it cannot be given a sense by*
             affirmation. Indeed its sense is just what is affirmed. And the same applies to
             negation, etc.

Comments: The sense of a proposition (or a metaphor) is an automatic consequence
             of its ergative formulation (subjugating its expression to the very words
             through which it is iterated) and has nothing to do with its categorical
             content apart from this. As language disguises thought, so propositional
             logic disguises memory. There would be no language apart from the sense
             imparted in its disguising of affairs; there would be no history without
             the special sense of drama imparted in its frustration of memories. If
             memory were nothing but the crystal-clear recounting of facts as they
             happened, there would be no sense at all. The world would be nonsense.

4.121   *Propositions cannot represent logical form: it is mirrored in them. What finds*
             its reflection in language, language cannot represent. What expresses itself in
             language, we cannot express by means of language.
             Propositions show the logical form of language.
             They display it.

Comment: This proposition is a "no brainer"; it shows what language cannot say by
             saying what language cannot show, describes accurately the way in which
             language cannot describe itself. Hence it performs in its own articulation
             the conjunction of self-agency and self-revelation that characterizes the

sense of what Wittgenstein calls "logic," and so stands at the very apex of his effort to define philosophy as the art of refining the proposition. In effect, 4.121 is the proposition that contains all other propositions (by "propositioning" them), a sort of assignational brothel.

The (colossal) implications of this are apt to be missed or overlooked unless considered very carefully, and in detail. What Wittgenstein has done is to universalize the boundary conditions of the proposition into a substitute for the adequate or veridical perception of the world around us. We do not, in other words, connect the words or sign-values that make up our world directly or realistically with percepts in the sensed world around us, but rather with other words and sign-values. We isolate ourselves with language, and then isolate language with ourselves. So that the resulting combinations (word–word rather than word–thing) represent by analogy at best an apocryphal "something" that is supposed to exist outside of us, out there in the world. We "echolocate" a world of imaginal percepts, the things of saying things, outside of us like bats, finding their way around very real obstacles that are nonetheless intangible. Save by sound. We live in a microcosm, a "bubble of reflection," perceiving our own reflections (and the reflections of our thoughts) on the inside surface of the bubble, like the self-perceiving isolates described in Gottfried Wilhelm Leibniz's "Monadology" ([1714] 1989).

If we follow the implications of this proposition (and of the "Monadology" as well) to their logical conclusion, there is nothing to prevent the following scenario: there is no such thing as a past, or a present, or a future, a legitimate or illegitimate set of memories or antecedents connecting to a past—no individual or collective history—and no credible anticipatory expectations abridging such designs to a future state. There is only a single, all-encompassing holography of experience—a perfect mutual occlusion of part and whole in any conceivable contingency—that expresses the "internal property" of all possible circumstances, a figure–ground reversal of being and mind. The problem with this scenario is that, as with "Monadology" (or Plato's "cave" analogy), there is no empirical means of either confirming or denying it. In a manner of speaking, it is like the perfect, suppressed ergative existence (action registered and amplified in a passive state), or the "who's in control" dilemma that bedevils the marital state. Understood in this way, "human sentience" or whatever else one might call it is, like the internet, the perfect media fantasy; it gives the illusion of control over others while one is being controlled absolutely by the internalized context-adjustment program of the internet.

In the opening of his "Eighth Duino Elegy," the poet Rainer Maria Rilke offers a startling alternative to human "sentience" in the suggestion that, contrary to its human counterpart, the animal's face expresses what is outside of it, rather than what is inside of it. I translate freely from his (German) text:

> With all its eyes the creature
> sees openness. Only our eyes
> are turned around and arranged
> like traps set around the way out, the exit.
> What really is out there, we know from
> the animal's face alone; because we force
> even the very young child to turn
> its perception inside-out, so that it sees
> the form and shaping of things backward—not
> the openness that is so deep in the animal's
> face, free as it is of death.
> We see death alone; the free animal
> has its downfall always behind it
> and God in front, and when it goes
> it goes straight into eternity, the way springs
> run. We have never, not even for a single day
> had that pure space before us, into which
> flowers endlessly open upon.

4.125   *The existence of an internal relation between possible situations expresses itself in language by means of an internal relation between the propositions representing them.*

Comment: Propositions, in other words, "communicate" with one another by internal resonance only, a kind of vibrational logicality (as Wittgenstein would have it) that resembles the sympathetic vibrations of crystals (or crickets). The match is so perfect that our idea of "communication" would be beside the point. This brings up the intriguing question about the "situations" represented in (a) the engineering design of a machine as manifest in the gears, levers, and other mechanical components of the material that makes it up, and (b) the energy-configuration that "embodies" the working of the machine once it is set in motion. Clearly the relation between these two situations is not one of cause and effect, for each of the two situations models itself upon the other in an immediate way. Just as (in the way that) the arbitrage of language conventions models itself on the occasions of its usage (propositions), and vice versa, or in the way that different crystals (or crickets) model one another via the resonance between them.

Wittgenstein was a cricket-shaman.

4.1251   *Here we have the answer to the vexed question "whether all relations are internal or external."*

Comment: This proposition dispels the illusion that anything could be gained by making either telepathy or the much-vaunted "intersubjectivity" of the phenomenologists the proper medium of conventional communication. For they are not information per se, but information about information—that is, revelations that make no sense unless we are aware of the concrete lexical items to which they refer. The key, as in Proposition 4.125, is "expresses itself in language," because without a referentiality to the things outside of it, communication is just simply "inside dope," however subtle its implications and innuendos. "We have evidence that the *Iliad* and *Odyssey* were not written by the Homer we know so well, but by another Greek of the same name." That would be the intersubjective proof of the authorship of the two epics.

My experience with telepaths (they do exist, and I am not one of them) is that they never bother to tell you anything that is not intended as a stunning revelation. Since ordinary humor offers the same advantage without the necessity of overcommitting oneself, one has to wonder about these people.

5.131   *If the truth of one proposition follows from the truth of others, this finds expression in relations in which the forms of the propositions stand to one another: nor is it necessary for us to set up these relations between them by combining them with one another in a single proposition; on the contrary, the relations are internal, and their existence is an immediate result of the existence of the propositions.*

Comment: As Abraham Lincoln once put it (in the Lincoln–Douglas debates):
                "Mighty big shuckin' for such a small nubbin."

                By setting up the standard of internal versus external alone as the
                sole criterion by which relations among the propositions may be as-
                sessed, this proposition stands as the vindication of the logical form
                displayed in G. Spencer-Brown's *Laws of form* (1969). In that work the
                author uses a notational schema consisting of brackets and parentheses
                to demonstrate his point: the relations of containment (inclusion) and
                decontainment (exclusion) alone control the circumstances of any rela-
                tions among propositions, which would either contain one another or
                exclude one another for all the sense they might make.

                Hence the conclusion reached in this way by both Wittgenstein and
                Spencer-Brown is both analytical and synthesizing at once, and not logi-
                cal, philosophical, or even psychological so much as it is topological—
                one thinks of the topological figures known as the Klein bottle, which
                contains its own decontainment of itself, and the Möbius strip, which
                decontains its own decontainment.

5.132   *If* p *follows from* q, *I can make an inference from* q *to* p, *deduce* p *from* q.
                The nature of the inference can be gathered only from the two propositions.
                They themselves are the only possible justification of the inference.
                "Laws of inference," which are supposed to justify inferences, as in the works of
                Frege and Russell, have no sense, and would be superfluous.

Comment: By obviating ("anticipating and disposing of") the very possibility of
                building tree-like structures of logical inference and antecedence among
                propositions, and anything else that might even remotely stand for
                them, this proposition delivers the coup de grâce to the whole series
                of gargantuan frauds developed in the mid-twentieth century under
                the aegis of what was then called "logical positivism." These include the
                unlamented "ethnoscience" and "ethnosemantic" approaches to cultural
                categorization ("classification"), as well as the blasé "constructionist"
                and "deconstructionist" fantasies that followed upon their dismissal. As
                Wittgenstein points out here, however, all real and potential relations
                of a given proposition to any other propositions (or, we may add, clas-
                sificatory categorization to other categories, or cultural context to other
                contexts) are contained within the (propositional) implications of that

proposition (or cultural categorization, or context) itself, so that any attempt to superimpose ad-hoc logical designs of order upon them would be superfluous at best, intellectual masturbation at worst.

5.133   *All deductions are made a priori.*

Comment: If each separate proposition contains, as a matter of its own self-definition as such, its own unique field of logical predication, then any deduction or inference made within that field simply reiterates its premises, and returns to the "ground zero" a priori nature of the original ("a priori = original"). Likewise, any deduction or inference made outside of that field of predication, regardless of any supposed relation to it or anything else, is also a priori. (Example: non sequitur, "does not follow," is also a relation, and attaches to the proposition in a very original—a priori—way.) This last observation is very unorthodox (e.g., counterintuitive) and may give the reader some trouble on that account. If so, then please give close attention to the following two propositions.

5.134   *One elementary proposition cannot be deduced from another.*

Comment: If it could, it would not be an elementary proposition but a derivative proposition.

5.135   *There is no possible way of making an inference from the existence of one situation to the existence of another, entirely different situation.*

Comment: This proposition follows from the previous one (i.e., 5.134) by virtue of the same logic of non sequitur intransitivity through which that previous one in its turn was uninferred from the one previous to it, in a noninferential chain of nondeductive reasoning (or unreasonable facsimile thereof) that has all the candor and charm of a double negative. In other (non) words, what appears to be non sequitur or internally self-contradictory in the (apparently illogical) sequence of these propositions bears immediately upon the reasoning by which the double negative is nominally disallowed from normal discourse. This is the assumption of an automatic cause-and-effect (deductive-inferential) relation between two such qualifiers modifying the subject (and thus each other) in a linear syntactic sequence. Should

we demur, and reject this commonplace half-truth by visualizing the two
negations in a different perspective, it appears that the two negations
may have been intended in parallel with one another (instead of at cross-
purposes), and thus grant a double motivation to the subject. Like two
towers at opposite ends of a suspension bridge, which both support the
way between them, as vividly evoked in Hart Crane's poem "To Brooklyn
Bridge": ". . .and of the curveship lend a myth to God."

Not only does this second option reflect the preferred position of our
predecessor language, Middle English, which did allow double negatives,
and therefore retained a healthy skepticism regarding cause and effect,
but it also justifies the internal cohesion of the propositions from 5.131
to 5.1361, inclusive, which stand in an exactly parallel relation to one another. It is as though they were all saying the same thing, which they are,
and to which fact Wittgenstein would doubtless refer as their internal
cohesion.

5.136   *There is no causal nexus to justify such an inference .*

Comment: QED. (*Quod erat demonstrandum.*) In an optimal bridge or other structure, the weight or load it carries is as much supported by the structure
as the structure is by the load itself. R. Buckminster Fuller called this
principle "tensegrity," and it is equivalent to the action of self-modeling
in the case of a language, a machine, a myth ("obviation"), or a proposition. In every case it is at best tangential to the causal nexus, which is at
best an irrationalization.

5.1361   *We cannot infer the events of the future from those of the present.*
Superstition is nothing but belief in the causal nexus.

Comment: The causal nexus, or assumed cause-and-effect relation, is a contradiction
in terms, in that it both presumes a relation (e.g., a gap within the event
as it happens) that could not exist as such, and disposes of that relation as
the very means of its existence. Does the spark jump the gap, or the gap
"jump" the spark? To be effective at all, either in a mechanical sense or a
logical-deductive one, the cause and the effect would have to be one and
the same action. But if it were admitted that this is the case—that is, if
the necessary interval between causality and effectiveness were admitted

openly as a fiction—we would lose the ability to represent (e.g., imagine) any sort of action—be it mental or physical—in a linear sequence.

But if it were admitted that not only superstition, but logical inference and the effectiveness of (natural or cultural) physical action were "nothing but belief in the causal nexus," what about disbelief in the causal nexus, or even partial (skeptical) belief in the causal nexus? We may take humor or irony as the case in point here, for a joke or humorous communication always gives one the effect first (as in the "set-up" or initial picturing of the scenario of a joke), and then surprises one (in what is called the punchline) with some unlikely or unsuspected cause as the thing that makes the joke funny, or the irony quizzical. Inverting the causal nexus, or cause-and-effect sequency, upon itself is in fact the signature virtue of the humorous technique, if only for the fact that it encourages one to doubt one's own convictions, a doubt that is all the more remarkable for the fact that a causal nexus reversed upon itself is still a causal nexus. Would you believe it?

Still, the relation of humor to invention (innovation, particularly technological) is illustrated by the fact that both rely on surprising the subject with some previously unlikely or unsuspected cause. ("The reason our detergent cleans best is that it produces a new kind of shiny bubbles! This is important because in the old days the housewife had to shine all the bubbles by hand!!") In the product-fantasy world of the late twentieth century, advertising took the place of automation ("works by itself") as the main humor by which things worked. In the "cyberspace" world of the early twenty-first century, the nexus ("superstition") automatically inverted on itself—things started to be about advertising instead of advertising being about things. (This made visible the "funny" side of Wittgenstein.)

5.1362   *The freedom of the will consists in the impossibility of knowing actions that still lie in the future. We could know them only if causality were an inner necessity like that of logical inference—the connexion between knowledge and what is known is that of logical necessity.*

          ("A knows that p *is the case" has no sense of* p *as a tautology.)*

Comment: The causal nexus (a tautology, since "cause" and "effect" both refer to the same thing) is a mere metaphor of action, and has the same logical necessity as a metaphor. Only if it were known for a fact that the moon is not a lovely woman would it make sense to assert that the moon is a lovely woman. A trope or metaphor, like a proposition, asserts an identity (tautology) in cases where such an identity is known to be contrary to fact. It makes a better lie of the knowable truth than the knowable truth could make of it, and in this sense (which is that of sense itself), language goes in deadly peril whenever it talks about itself. (Danger of talking itself out of its own lexicon.)

Here we come to the point of closure between the trope and the proposition, for both are committed to (and motivated by) the comparison of language with itself. That is, in both cases normally disparate parts of the lexicon, or disparate modes of intentionality ("free will") as articulated in language, are compared in their identification, and identified in their comparison.

Hence the fact that the world has many different languages does not mean they were all the same once (e.g., that they all developed from a common rootlanguage), or that they will all be the same at some time in the future ("evolution" of a common end language). For the comparison between languages (translation) is as much a condition for their separate existences as such as the comparison among parts of a language is for its separate existence as a language per se.

A language that followed completely from its own rules and regularities would be a pure tautology, and make no sense. A language that followed completely from its own sense would be a pure hypocrisy (like certain forms of phenomenology and New Age philosophy), and have no rules.

5.143   *Contradiction is that common factor of propositions which no proposition has in common with another. Tautology is the common factor of all propositions that have nothing in common with one another.*

Contradiction, one might say, vanishes outside all propositions: tautology vanishes inside them.

Contradiction is the outer limit of propositions: tautology is the insubstantial point at their center.

Comment: The origin of language itself may be said to have begun with the act of self-comparison (comparing one part of language with another is comparing language with the world of its referentiality). People began to compare disparate things with one another, and then realized they had nothing to compare, and no way to compare them. Imagine the following Ur-scenario:

"I said that."

"How could you say that when you really meant this?"

"Well maybe because your this is my that."

"Prove it."

"Look it up in the contradictionary!"

5.156   *It is in this way that probability is a generalization. It involves a general description of a propositional form.*

We use probability in default of certainty—if our knowledge of a fact is not indeed complete, but we do know something about its form.

(A proposition may well be an incomplete picture of a certain situation, but it is always a complete picture of something.)

A probability proposition is a sort of excerpt from other propositions.

Comment: Wrong! A probability proposition is not an excerpt; it is the general case of all propositions. For if our knowledge of the fact stated in and as the proposition (the picture of its picture, as it were) were indeed complete— that is, if it were specific rather than general—there would be no need to state it as a proposition, for it would be a tautology, and, as per 5.143, would vanish inside of itself. Just as a trope or metaphor must always be a wager, with its truth or falsehood up for grabs, so a proposition must always be hazarded against the possibility of its failure as such.

This is an extremely important point, which we met with earlier (2.172) in the inability of a picture to depict itself. It bears upon the centrality of intent or intentionality to all human action and expression. Uncertainty is the ground of all action, and ignorance of all knowledge, as Ursula Le Guin puts it in *The left hand of darkness*: "If it were proven that there is no God there would be no religion. . . . But also if it were proven there is a God, there would be no religion" ([1969] 2017: 70). Religion lives in the hazarding of intent between these two alternatives. Absolute certainty is only useful when one is uncertain about its outcome. So is a proposition.

We might term 5.156 "The Schrödinger Proposition," for it invalidates the possibility of empirical proof in the case of propositional knowledge, which is not "falsifiable." As such this proposition obviates ("anticipates and disposes of") the whole discussion between 5.2 and 5.6 in the *Tractatus*, which we shall dismiss.

This brings us to cats. The entire cat family, remarkably consistent in its DNA, has evolved by pretending "no cat" to its prey, and projecting this dissimulation upon its whole environment. It is the "no cat" projector, and when the prey becomes convinced by this "stalking" procedure, the cat pounces. The payoff comes at the end of the cat's life, when the creature actually attains the condition (e.g., no cat) that its practice has heretofore only simulated. And once that condition ("ground zero") is achieved, the cat-animal simply pounces back from the other side and becomes some cat again, (Ever wonder where all those cats come from?) The same applies to propositions, and likewise metaphors. Ever wonder where they come from?

5.6   *The limits of my language mean the limits of my world.*

Comment: According to Victor Zuckerkandl, who argued that music, and not speech, was the primary unifying factor in human being, the limits of language are too intimately connected to its being as such to be normally visible. In his book *Man the musician*, he observes that:

> The limits of language does not imply the existence of a domain inaccessible to language. No such domain exists. Nothing actually or potentially relevant to human existence is beyond the grasp of language: the domain of the word is limitless. The limit beyond which words cannot go is their own delimiting activity. The limit of language is its being a limit. However broad or narrow the limits it may trace, there is one thing it never reaches: the delimited. . . . It is what is closest to us, manifestly present in everything that is not an intellectual or a linguistic fiction. (Zuckerkandl 1973: 65–66)

In other words it is not the etymological or formal linguistic character of the word that obscures its limiting capabilities, but the very fact of its being there in the first place. Concealment of its real content or subject is as much a function of language as communication itself, for what is communicated is in no small part the fact of that concealment, like a secret kept by language from itself.

5.61   *Logic pervades the world: the limits of the world are also its limits.*
So we cannot say in logic, "the world has this in it, and this, but not that."
For that would appear to presuppose that we were excluding certain possi-
bilities, and this cannot be the case, since it would require that logic would go
beyond the limits of the world: for only in that way could it view those limits
from the other side as well.
We cannot think what we cannot think, so we cannot think what we cannot
say either.

Comment: Logic cannot, in other words, be identified with the lexicon, but must also include all the possible permutations and combinations of its inventory, its metaphoric potential, so to speak. Logic is like a mirror that inverts the significational potential of its dictionary-like inventory, fixes internal as well as external limits to our ability to know and say things.

5.621   *The world and life are one.*

Comment: We do not live in the world: we live a description of the world, and how and why that description is made, and in what it consists, are totally beside the point of this. Life experience may extend or alter that description, but does not change its essential nature as a description. The fact of description imposes an internal as well as an external boundary on the life experience we call the world.

5.63   *I am my world (the microcosm).*

Comment: The description of the world is a small-scale model or miniature—in other words, a microcosm—of the unknowable reality that lies beyond it, and that description attempts to copy for its own purposes. To identify oneself with the microcosm means that one is the description of a description of a description.

5.631   *There is no such thing as the subject that thinks or entertains ideas.*

If I wrote a book called The world as I found it, *I should have to include a report on my body, and should have to say which parts were subordinate to my will, and which were not, etc. This being a method of isolating the subject, or rather of showing in an important sense that there is no subject; for it alone could not be mentioned in that book.*

Comment: Cf. Jorge Luis Borges (1998: 126): "In a riddle whose answer is chess, what is the one word that may never be mentioned?" The subject, by analogy, must necessarily be excluded from any discussion of the subject, if only because it defies objectification in those terms. Put in Borges's terms, this means it is impossible to proposition the subject and not checkmate oneself. This proposition is a direct confession on Wittgenstein's part of the central role played by the agentive subject/object shift in the epistemology of the *Tractatus*. The whole work is based on an automatic and taken-for-granted (e.g., invisible to its author) transformational subject/object shift.

The acid test of any Wittgenstein proposition is to apply its lesson back again to itself. Hence whatever else it may be or mean, a word is an objectification such that whatever it denotes, connotes, or in any way represents is automatically subjected by it. Hence to be subjected is to have a meaning or significance of some sort in consequence of its subjugated, or in other words passive, status. Thus meaningfulness and subjectivity are two different words that describe the same thing. How is this lesson to be applied to itself?

When, as in this case, we are obliged to reobjectify what is already an objectification, we inadvertently perform a subject/object shift, force the original objectification into a passive, or subjugated, status. In other words, we unwittingly engineer a double comparison between subjectification and objectification: the subject of an object is the object of its own subjectification.

Hence the otherwise enigmatic self-referentiality of this proposition (which might be called an assignation on that account). The question of whether Wittgenstein used the facts of symbolic representation ("logic") to demonstrate the power of double comparison, or simply used the means of double comparison to demonstrate the facts of symbolic representation, is itself an example of the double-comparative method. In this respect the double comparison, like the version of it used by Kurt

Gödel to demonstrate his famous Proof, is both self-constituting and self-modeling—it signifies what it represents by representing not only what it signifies, but also how it came to signify it in that way. Its causes are its effects and its effects are its causes, like the Fibonacci sequence in mathematics, in which each successive number is the sum of the previous two.

5.632   *The subject does not belong to the world: rather, it is a limit of the world.*

Comment: This follows directly from the precondition of the subject/object shift and the logic of double comparison. In order to know, recognize, or even speak of a phenomenal description of the world, we must necessarily objectify it. There are no unobjectified elements in the human inventory. But by the act of analysis, by acknowledging that what we normally take for granted as facts and realities of the world around us are really only parts of a description, we automatically predicate them as subjects of discussion, and thereby transpose them outside the world that the description is supposed to describe. As projections of our perceived world of tangible realities, they are necessarily outside of that world. (A highly provocative point, for it directly controverts the commonplace notion that meaningfulness or thought takes place inside the world, or even inside the brain!)

5.633   *Where in the world is a metaphysical subject to be found?*
           You will say that this is exactly like the gash of the eye and the visual field. But
           really you do not see the eye.
           And nothing in the visual field allows you to infer that it is seen by the eye.

Comment: By analogy, then, nothing in the described world allows you to infer that it is only the object of a description. This proposition, probably the most beautiful one in the *Tractatus*, sounds the death knell of the scientific method and the credibility of positivism itself, which will now have to be called projectivism.
           The Kwakiutl Indians of British Columbia speak of a mythical sea-monster that this proposition shows to be real. The monster, called the Sisiutl, is like a giant serpent with a head at each end of its body. Thus in order to attack its victim, the Sisiutl must turn its two heads to face each

other and thus inadvertently peer into its own eyes. But, as the Kwakiutl say, any creature capable of staring into its own eye is gifted on the spot with incredible wisdom. So it realizes it does not want to devour the victim after all, gives it a gift, and goes away.

My Barok congeners in New Ireland would call this gift "the reciprocity of perspectives."

5.634   *This is connected with the fact that no part of our experience is at the same time a priori.*
Whatever we see could be other than it is.
Whatever we can describe at all could be other than it is.
There is no a priori order of things.

Comment: A priori prioritizes a necessary beginning point, like a first principle from which other principles may be adduced, or an original state of affairs from which the present state may be said to derive, or in other words, an anticipation of something that has already taken place. The classic instance of this would be an origin myth or creation account in which time is reversed and the actual a priori or point of origination comes at the end rather than the beginning of the narrative. The past, in other words, must always be anticipated—that is, postponed to the very end—if only to preserve the credibility of the account. What this means, of course, is that a valid a priori must always be anticipated, not only in its mythic derivation from other things or other states of affairs, but even in its logical priority, and thus made contingent and tentative, if only by the fact that is has no subject at all.

5.64   *Here it can be seen that solipsism, when its implications are followed out strictly, coincides with pure realism. The self of solipsism shrinks to a point without extension, and there remains the reality coordinated with it.*

Comment: This proposition can neither be accepted nor refuted. A solipsist is convinced that they have invented the world around them, so that a perfectly self-confident solipsist would be satisfied with this knowledge, and never have to confess the fact to others. Thus the only solipsists we ever hear from are those who need independent confirmation of their stupendous achievement: "I invented you, didn't I?" If they say "yes," their

confirmation is not independent, for it is based on your having invented them, and if they say "no," they forfeit their credibility as a witness.
Hence we can conclude that if Wittgenstein were a true solipsist, he
would never have written this book to serve as independent confirmation
of that fact, and if he were a false solipsist (as most of us are), I would
never have written this comment to deny confirmation. Conclusion: the
claim of solipsism belongs to the set of double-proportional comparisons, like Gödel's Proof, and is both true and false at the same time. Like
Gödel's Proof, one of its long-term side-effects is paranoia.

6.1   *The propositions of logic are tautologies.*

Comment: What differentiates a mathematical equation from the commonplace
                tautology, or needless repetition of an idea, is that, like metaphor, it con-
                flates together two different descriptions of the same phenomenon, and
                uses that conflation to synthesize a previously unsuspected perspective.
                Now this is exactly the relation that the propositions of the *Tractatus*
                have both to themselves and to one another, so that their apparently
                tautological continuity masks an entirely novel and deliberately counter-
                intuitive philosophical perspective.

6.111   *All theories that make a proposition of logic appear to have content are false.*
                One might think, for example, that the words "true" and "false" signified two
                properties among other properties, and then it would seem to be a remarkable
                fact that every proposition possessed one of these properties. On this theory it
                seems to be anything but obvious, just as, for instance, the proposition "all roses
                are either yellow or red" would not sound obvious even if it were true. Indeed,
                the logical proposition acquires all the characteristics of a proposition of natu-
                ral science and that is the sure sign that it has been construed wrongly.

Comment: This proposition is not only self-modeling, it is also self-defining
                and self-proving. What it shows is that at this point in his argument
                Wittgenstein is no longer using the subject/object shift to make his
                point, but is actually being used by it. In other words he is engineer-
                ing a double comparison between a proposition in natural science and
                a proposition in logic to make his case, and in so doing he becomes the
                subject rather than the object of his discourse.

Thus, all he needed to say was: *A proposition of natural science depends on evidence for its confirmation, whereas a proposition in logic depends on confirmation for its evidence.*

6.121   *The propositions of logic demonstrate the logical properties of propositions by combining them to form propositions that say nothing.*
          This method could also be called the zero-method. In a logical proposition, propositions are brought into equilibrium with one another, and the state of equilibrium then indicates what the logical constitution of those propositions must be.

Comment: The zero-term in mathematical notation serves as a metaphor for "no integer being there." Lexically, that is, it shares with other metaphors the property of being a contradiction in terms, something that says what it does not mean and does so by meaning what it does not say. This further expedites the point of 6.111 by showing that a double comparison is absolutely necessary to make sense of nothing.

6.1222   *This throws some light on the question why logical propositions cannot be confirmed by experience any more than they can be refuted by it. Not only must a proposition of logic be irrefutable by any possible experience, but it must also be unconfirmable by any possible experience.*

Comment: This proposition can be taken generally as the denial or negation of any possible empirical methodology, such as the "scientific method," insofar as logical propositions are concerned, and that is doubtless the way in which Wittgenstein intended it. In that sense, the proposition is like the negative of the photographic print of what we call "empiricism." Nonetheless, empiricism is not positivism, and a negative shows just as much information as the positive print that is developed from it, and in that sense a logical proposition is not without informative value, for it does carry the value of the information it posits. Even though that information must be about itself.

          Here, however, we encounter another kind of problem, for we must experience a proposition (if only in the act of reading it) before we can know what it is about, especially if it is only about itself (like an equation, for instance, or a myth). And experiencing a proposition, by reading it or in any other way, is necessarily and ipso facto the same thing as confirming it by experience (for if we were to confirm it by some other experience, that other experience would have to be enough like the one we were confirming to ensure the validity of the comparison). As though to amend Heraclitus: "You shall not go down to the same river even once."

6.123   *Clearly the laws of logic cannot in their turn be subject to the laws of logic.*
(There is not, as Russell thought, a special law of contradiction for each "type": one law is enough, since it is not applied to itself.)

Comment: Even if they may be about themselves (e.g., in the way that an equation, or a metaphor, or a myth, is about itself) they do not describe, confirm, or allow one to experience the way in which they are about themselves, and so they are not subject to themselves. That is, they merely state what they state, without making that statement contingent upon itself. Clearly a proposition cannot be about the way it came to be a proposition in the first place, any more than an embryo could make itself pregnant with itself. For an embryo to procreate itself would require it to become an embryo of an embryo, and if the laws of logic followed this course they would never see the light of day.

6.1231   *The mark of a logical proposition is not general validity.*
To be general means no more than to be accidentally valid for all things. An ungeneralized proposition can be tautological just as well as a generalized one.

Comment: The phrase "accidentally valid" implies that the propositions obey an internal logic that is not necessarily reflected in standardized validation procedures. We must remember that the *Tractatus* was written almost fifty years before the discovery of fractal mathematics and its idealization in the form of chaos science. A fractal mathematician would want to amend Wittgenstein and point out that the propositions are in fact fractal iterations of one another (reiteration = tautology), sharing the same basic organizing principle, but each articulating it in a different way.

6.124   *The propositions of logic describe the scaffolding of the world, or rather they represent it. They have no "subject matter." They presuppose that names have meaning and elementary propositions sense; and that is their connexion with*

the world. It is clear that something about the world must be indicated by the
fact that certain combinations of symbols—whose essence involves the posses-
sion of a definite character—are tautologies. This contains the decisive point.
We have said that some things are arbitrary in the symbols that we use and
that some things are not. In logic it is only the latter that express: but that
means that logic is not a field in which we express what we wish with the help
of signs, but rather one in which the nature of the absolutely necessary signs
speaks for itself. If we know the logical syntax of any sign language, then we
have already been given all the propositions of logic.

Comment: This is the most open admission of the necessity of the subject/object
             shift and its role as the medium of symbolic communication in the whole
             text. It is through our very attempts to control them, make them obedi-
             ent to our will, that symbols (signs) control us, make their users obedient
             to their logic. It is clear that by overemphasizing the purely tautological
             implications of the subject/object shift, Wittgenstein was overlooking
             the fact that the double-comparative subject/object shift is more than a
             mere philosophical exercise—that it is a technology for turning a world-
             view into a world. A literal unpacking of a holographic symbolic order
             into the information necessary for a descriptive knowledge of the world
             of experience. In his book *The holographic universe*, Michael Talbot puts it
             this way:

> Holography possesses a fantastic capacity for information storage.
> By changing the angle by which the two lasers strike a piece of pho-
> tographic film, it is possible to record many different images on the
> same surface. Any image thus recorded can be retrieved simply by
> illuminating the film with a laser beam possessing the same angle as
> the original two beams. (1991: 21)

By analogy, then, a single world-image, such as that of the *Tractatus*,
can serve as a scaffolding for a whole world of information by means of
holographic (e.g., fractally self-iterating) imagery and imagistic information retrieval. The propositions have no "subject matter," any more than a
scaffolding is the building it was set up to construct. It is remarkable that
Wittgenstein did not consciously use the concept of holography here, in
the sense of an absolute identity between part and whole, but it is clear

that the mutual implications of the propositions, taken as fractal iterations, constitute a single image.

6.13   *Logic is not a body of doctrine, but a mirror-image of the world.*
        Logic is transcendental.

Comment: It was Bateson who pointed out that when you look in a mirror, you are looking at the back of an image (you see the back right through the perfectly transparent front), and that the mirror view's transposition of left and right is a direct consequence of this. Hence logic's mirroring of the world is a direct translation of an optical principle into a logical one, itself an irrefutable instance of the hegemony of the double-proportional syllogism. When a subject looks in a mirror, they see an object composed of their own retroversion. More properly, then, this proposition should read: *Logic is a figure–ground reversal of the world.*

6.24   *The method by which mathematics arrives at its equations is the method of substitution.*
        For equations express the substitutability of two expressions, and, starting from a number of equations, we advance to new equations by substituting different expressions in accordance with the equations.

Comment: This suggests a performative proposition, one that actually "propositions" its subject, as if to say "an equal sign is Euclid having sex." Substitution is the performative basis not only of mathematics, but also of narrative, temporal reckoning, and even of meaning itself: in narrative we substitute one mythic element for another (episode, attribute, character, etc.) in order to generate a story line or plot, one countable unit (second, minute, hour, day) for another in order to record the passage of time, one word or idea for another to provide the basis for metaphor and hence the inception of meaning. Beyond this we substitute one form of substitution itself for another in eliciting the evidence for an experiential world. Thus we keep the secret of significance from itself, largely because we have substituted language for thought, symbol for reality, and substitution itself for natural reality.

From a totally unbiased perspective, substitutions based on other substitutions constitute our way of life: What is anthropology for the anthropologist or logic for Wittgenstein but the substitution of a fantasy lifestyle for an unconscionable reality of dismal routines, ad hoc compromises, and noncommittal resolutions?

6.36111   *Kant's problem about the right hand and the left hand, which cannot be made to coincide, exists even in two dimensions. indeed, it exists in one-dimensional space*

$$---O—X—X—O---$$
$$\quad\quad a \quad\quad b$$

in which the two congruent figures, a *and* b, *cannot be made to coincide unless they are moved out of this space. The right hand and the left hand are in fact completely congruent, it is quite irrelevant that they cannot be made to coincide.*
A right-hand glove could be put on the left hand if it could be turned round in four-dimensional space.

Comment: The blind leading the blind. Kant was a basically asymmetrical thinker: what he knew about symmetry could quite literally fit in the palm of the hand. Just watch: a glove cut to fit the right hand will not fit over the left hand, and vice versa, *but* if the palms of the two hands are pressed together, a glove cut to fit *either* hand will fit over them both. (Note: this observation is also a refutation of another one of Kant's asymmetrical prodigies: the Categorical Imperative.)

6.371   *The whole modern conception of the world is founded on the illusion that the so-called laws of nature are the explanations of natural phenomena.*

Comment: The minute one tries to explain them, they become laws of culture instead—that is, mere projections of a self-conceived ability to explain. For nature itself is entirely innocent of either the need to explain or the ability to explain, as it is of number, quality, quantity, or even abstraction itself. "Nature" did not come with a book of instructions: instead of explaining something it creates it on its own authority (this is probably why most of its creatures are extinct).

6.373   *The world is independent of my will.*

Comment: Wrong question! The real question would be whether my will is inde-
            pendent of the world or not. For in fact everything I could wish for,
            ignore, or not wish for is a product of my contingency to the world of
            experience, and if I could experience nothing else I could know nothing
            else, either, and so will or wish for nothing else. But dependency in this
            case is necessarily a two-way (reciprocal) relation: the world is as much
            dependent on my will as my will is dependent on it, and Wittgenstein
            loses again by ignoring the subject/object shift.

6.41   *The sense of the world must lie outside the world. In the world everything is as
            it is, and everything happens as it does happen: in it no value exists—and if it
            did exist, it would have no value.*
            *If there is any value that does have value, it must lie outside the whole sphere of
            what happens and is the case. For all that happens and is the case is accidental.
            What makes it non-accidental cannot lie within the world, since if it did it
            would be itself accidental.*
            It must lie outside the world.

Comment: Compare with Victor Turner's equally transcendent definition of ritual
            as "expressing what cannot be thought of, in view of thought's subjuga-
            tion to essences" (1975: 187).
                A field anthropologist who has merged so completely with the life-
            ways of the people they are investigating that they may as well be one of
            them has lost the critical distance necessary to objectify those lifeways as
            an entity apart from their own participation in it. The sense or meaning
            of those lifeways is then taken for granted as a part of the "culture" they
            belong to, and can make no sense outside of that context. A culture whose
            sense is an integral part of it is beyond comparison or contrast, and in that
            sense is no culture at all. Thus the sense of a culture must necessarily exist
            outside of a culture in order for that culture to be recognized as such.
                By analogy a word that had the same sense as the thing it designates
            or "stands for" would lose the critical distance necessary for its referenti-
            ality and thereby its power to mean or signify. Thus the sense of a meta-
            phor must necessarily reside outside the range of the words that elicit it
            (e.g., outside the realm of Turner's "thinkable" essences), and so outside

of the lexicon. By contrast, the symbol that "stands for itself" offers a striking exception in that it models itself upon its own being there, and so contains its own meanings.

By so doing it offers an alternative, or "second attention" focus on the subject of meaning, and corresponds perfectly to Wittgenstein's description of the proposition as a self-defining tautology, incidentally proving the point I am trying to make here. Thus the sense of a double comparison cannot be part of that comparison without being compared to itself, and so contains its sense within its very formulation. Likewise the sense of a subject/object shift cannot be part of that shift without containing itself, becoming its own subject and its own object at one and the same time.

6.431   *So too at death the world does not alter, but comes to an end.*

Comment: That the world will end when my world ends would be a piece of errant mysticism but for the self-containment of sense in the subject/object shift. Death, in that context, is both its own subject (my world) and its own object (its world as a thing in itself), so that in the end there is absolutely no difference between my view of death and death's view of me. My view of death is mirrored in death's view of me, and vice versa.

6.4311   *Death is not an event in life: we do not live to experience death.*
                If we take eternity to mean not infinite temporal duration but timelessness,
                then eternal life belongs to those who live in the present.
                Our life has no end in just the way that our visual field has no limits.

Comment: The logic here is perfectly straightforward, and refers back to Proposition 5.633, which points out that the eye is necessarily excluded from its own visual field. So, by analogy, the now, or present moment, is excluded from all the limitations imposed by the duration or passage of time (it never has been any time but *now*, it never will be any time but *now*—and the *now* of my writing this be my witness, for it is eternally present).

6.4312   *Not only is there no guarantee of the temporal immortality of the human soul,*
                that is to say of its eternal survival after death, but, in any case, this assump-
                tion completely fails to accomplish the purpose for which it has always been

*intended. Or is some riddle solved by my surviving forever? Is not this eternal
life itself as much of a riddle as our present life? The solution of the riddle of life
in space and time lies outside space and time.*

*(It is certainly not the solution of any problems of natural science that is
required.)*

Comment: Because we are unaware of what awareness itself is, we are forced to conclude that being aware of the problem itself, which describes the present
moment, is quite enough for our purposes. When we go "back" in time
to try to experience the beginning of awareness's awareness of itself, we
are simply imitating our present-moment problem of trying to define
awareness, and projecting that effort backward in time, just as we must
project it forward, into the future, to imagine what death, or the cessa-
tion of awareness, will be like. Hence the human lifespan, measured by
its own awareness of being aware, is interminable in its own terms, being
asymptotic both in its approximation of our coming into the world and
in our taking leave of it, like a curve that gets closer and closer to a line
without ever touching it. As to whether some form of awareness precedes birth or follows after death, that is so much a part of the problem
of what awareness itself may be that a single answer is all that is required.

6.54   *My propositions serve as elucidations in the following way: anyone who understands me eventually recognizes them as nonsensical, when he has used
them—as steps—to climb up beyond them. (He must, so to speak, throw away
the ladder once he has climbed up it.)*

He must transcend these propositions, and then he will see the world aright.

Comment: The purpose of the propositions is neither to confirm nor to deny one
another and thus avoid the traditional philosophical trap of self-consist-
ency. Hence the "structure" of Wittgenstein's argument (Victor Turner
would call it as "antistructure") is self-obviational—anticipatory rather
than reflectional, more concerned with where it is going than with where
it has been. To obviate, according to the standard dictionary definition,
is "to anticipate and dispose of": obviation substitutes effect for cause,
change for stability, and end for beginning, and thus defines itself as a
philosophy of credible deniability: it keeps the secret of its own methodology from itself.

CHAPTER 3

Nonlinear causality

Nothing is more symptomatic of the intellectual stagnation of our times than the chains of unicausal implication that dominate everything from cosmology's "big bang" theory to evolutionary biology's commitment to individual lines of species descent. There can be no doubt that the culprit, the illusion of linear causality, is part of a general consensual pattern—perhaps a kind of folklore—linked to family trees, individual genealogies, chains of command, organizational tree-diagrams, etc., none of which have any counterpart in reality. Like other human fictions—numbers, abstractions, laws of nature—unicausality must be teased out of naturally occurring phenomena by ad hoc demonstrations and experiments, or else superimposed on them by authoritative dogmas. Nothing in nature or even human nature works that way.

Lest we forget, the whole idea of an inherent natural order is of our own making. But if linear causality-chains have no place in reality, neither do other linear series of implication like biographies or historical chronicles: in all cases determining influences converge, diverge, and intersect with one another at all angles. Just as in the diagraming of an obviation sequence. Notice that all points on the diagram (A, B, C, . . .), apices of triangles as they may be, are directly connected to one another by straight lines, regardless of whether the story line-narrative puts them in the past or future. From the standpoint of obviation they all exist equally in the same cross-connecting system, and the question of their temporal priority is an arbitrary one: they are all part of a nonlinear pattern of mutual implication.

There is another way of understanding this, but to make it work we must substitute elicitation (evocation) for causation (both are forms of implication). A metaphor or trope, taken in itself, is meaningless—it simply equates one word or thing with another, so that the interpreter is obliged to clarify the incongruity (e.g., the stated identity between two disparate things), by extending the process, eliciting another incongruity to take its place, thus turning the initial metaphor into a self-continuative analogical flow, a dovetailing of individual metaphors, so to speak, each successive one being a metaphor of the previous metaphor. To wit: "this is that, is that, is that," building an analogical supersaturation like an oil stain spreading over a piece of cloth; a self-inducing metaphor spread out. In this regard obviation corresponds to a nonlinear pattern of implication: it "grows," as Victor Zuckerkandl points out, "in a dimension perpendicular to time (1973: 191).

Linear causality, by contrast, is unthinkable and unworkable without its chronological timeline. Nonlinear causality works its magic within the presence rather than the passage of time, the "once upon a time" of storytelling. A myth or story, like a symphony, occupies a circumscribed gestalt, or organic timespan of its own, the kind of temporal reshaping of space to its own designs that Mikhail Bakhtin (1981) called a chronotope, literally a "timespace" in direct contradistinction to the "spacetime" of the physicists. Spacetime makes a discourse of the universe; timespace makes a universe of the discourse.

Just why is the format and technique of obviation important to a study of nonlinear causality? It is important because, unlike the examples of chiasmatic, or double-proportional, comparison (subject/object shift, remote intentional discourse, etc.) that I have used so far in this discussion, all of which, at most, depend on two figure–ground reversals, obviation depends on three to come full circle—that is, round out its chronotopic self-containment. The difference is an important one, because three-ness allows for the closure, the termination point of causal implication afforded by a Hegelian synthesis, whereas duality poses the danger of a never-ending dialectic exchange: thesis–antithesis–thesis–antithesis, and so on, to the crack of doom.

Obviation thereby offers a three-dimensional perspective on the workings of double-proportional comparison, and, as per its definition, "anticipates and disposes of" its subject, rendering its inner workings obvious in the process.

Pause here and reflect on this point: a causality that anticipates and disposes of its object is no causality at all. It is, quite simply, an obviation.

Thus in the following pages I shall proceed to obviate, rather than explicate, one of Papua New Guinea's most challenging indigenous ontological programs, the notorious *Amowkam*, or "Mother House," complex at Telefolip, located in the Star Mountains at the very geographical center of the island of New Guinea. As the reader shall come to understand, obviation makes more sense than explanation in that context.

THE CURSE OF THE MOUNTAIN OK

Until the appearance of Joel Robbins's *Becoming sinners* (2004) and Tony Crook's *Exchanging skin* (2007), Eytan Bercovitch's curse of the Mountain Ok—"that no one but Fredrik Barth shall write a book about the Mountain Ok"—had the status of a self-fulfilling prophecy. Usually ignored by the general public, and often disprized in favor of other, catchier trends and initiatives (read "dysfunctional academical cargo cults" for the late twentieth century), insightful synthesis in the social sciences does have its moments. As John Farella put it in his landmark study of Navajo religion, *The main stalk*: "When culture is 'lost,' as the anthropologists like to put it, or when it erodes, it is the synthetic knowledge or the meaning that goes first. Without this knowledge, nothing else in the culture, especially the ritual, can make any sense" (1984: 14).

The cryptonym "Ok" refers to a group of linguistically related peoples living at high altitude in the Star Mountains, so designated because many of their words end with the sound -*ok*. It has nothing whatever to do with the OK Corral, or with the shootout at the OK Corral, unless one pays attention to Barbara Jones (1980), whose friends at Imigabip told her, "We are cowboys," meaning they live lives of quiet desperation, or to Farella, who, as he once told me, was "raised as a cowboy." The peoples are also referred to as the min, deriving the generic designation from their suffix -*min* (a cognate of the Daribi -*bidi*), as in "Faiwolmin," "Urapmin," or "Telefolmin."

Hence the phrase "a Dodge City full of Wittgensteins" has more to do with epistemology and obviation than with the Earp brothers and Doc Holliday, and with a phenomenon that is a prodigy in its own right, neither anthropological nor indigenous, but rather, as W.B. Yeats would put it, woven of "the light and the half-light."

The anomaly I am speaking of here, the so-called "Afek religion of the Ok People of the Star Mountains," did not exist before exogenous investigators came on the premises, and will not persist long afterward. It had its moment of glory, like a neutron star, or like the "floating world" of blossom petals that Japanese poets write about, and will live forever on the pride of its own evanescence. It is an anomaly unparalleled in the history of anthropological reportage; nonetheless it is possible to list the attributes that made it appear that way.

1. Multiethnic, "transnational" religions, with a preestablished dogma, a permanent physical institutionalized base, and a centralized, hierarchical priesthood, are not supposed to exist in what we condescendingly called "tribal" societies, and in the absence of a dominant, secular, centralized state. Nonetheless this is just exactly what we find in the Mother House complex of the Afek religion, centered on the tightly restricted sacred village of Telefolip, ruled by a "queen," and, according to archaeologist Pamela Swadling, rebuilt on the same spot for the past four hundred years.

2. Ritualized knowledge and its teaching, elsewhere in Melanesia, is not supposed to be a thing in and of itself, and valued for its own sake; it is rather linked with age grading and the stages of the life-process, or at most to the revelatory procedures of spirit mediums and shamans. It is not supposed to engage heuristic or conceptual teaching devices identical to those of quantum mechanics (Schrödinger's cat, the Uncertainty Principle, the Doppler effect), ancient Greek philosophy (the aporiai of Zeno or Heraclitus or Plato's "cave" analogy), or Zen koan. Nonetheless, usages identical to every one of these have been put into practice as standard teaching devices for perhaps hundreds of years in the Mother House complex at Telefolip and its outlying nucleated epicenters, as at Faiwol (cf. Barth 1975; Jones 1980; Crook 2007). Probably the most comprehensive and certainly the most authoritative of these investigations was carried out by the ethnographer Dan Jorgensen at the Mother House complex at Telefolip, where the site of his house was pointed out to me with awe, near one of the sacred groves of Afek, the creatress.

3. Young, preprofessional "graduate students" as well as seasoned professionals, the "best and brightest" of their generation, are supposed to seek out

challenges for their abilities among peoples representing the exotic, the mysterious, or forbidden, if only as a sort of group therapy for a discipline driven to the brink of intellectual bankruptcy by decades of "same old same old" conceptual examples. They are not supposed to (a) return with a negative dissertation subject, or none at all, (b) disappear off the face of the earth, or (c) lose their spouse, their children, their job, and pass within a hair's breadth of being declared insane. Nonetheless, all of these things did happen to researchers into the Mother House complex, especially among the Faiwol, and it is for that reason that Tony Crook calls the place "the graveyard of anthropological careers." (pers. comm.)

4. Scientists, and even ordinary people, are not supposed to deviate from the established dogma of unicausal chains of event or happening, or from the illusion of a logical consistency that stems from such simplistic single cause/single effect sequences. As Gregory Bateson put it, "All that is required is that we ask not about the characteristics of lineal chains of cause and effect but about the characteristics of systems in which the chains of cause and effect are circular or more than circular" (1958: 288). The effect of the *ban* system of the Mother House was to shift the weight of emphasis from us to them, and from observation to explanation.

The indigenous word *ban* means "explanation," more likely something like "the interlocking verbal and imagistic demonstration of a basically synthesizing knowledge," or in other words, what Ludwig Wittgenstein would consider a propositional argument and Hegel a dialectical synthesis. To clarify further, the unifying effect of what we would call "explanation" is substituted for by the synthesis of new knowledge from what others would call "data." The Faiwol, or Faiwolmin, classically understood as the second ranked (in terms of ritual power) among the various ethnicities participating in the *ban* system, were studied, in temporal order, by Fredrik Barth (1975), in the isolated community of Baktaman, by Barbara Jones (1980), in the large community of Imigabip, and by Crook (2007) at Bolivip, historically the first Mountain Ok community to be contacted by outsiders. Barth's study was the first to give a complete perspective on the details of *ban* practice, and a glimpse into their almost uncanny originality; Jones's study, called "Consuming society," portrays the reality of a negative sociality at its most extreme—a society that actually consumes itself (forget Orwell and Spengler: the view presented in her field notes would give string theory nightmares!); Crook's study, with its brilliant evocation of chiasmatic "power-talk," shows the subtle and underdetermined foil by which the whole system operates, and basically resolves the legendary "problem of the Mountain Ok."

OBVIATION OF THE *BAN* SYSTEM

As so often in what are condescendingly called the "symbolic" aspects of the knowledge quest, the morphology of the sequence—its setup of stages or episodes in prospect of later ones and in retrospect of earlier ones—tells a better story about the narrative itself. Content follows form and in fact invades it, perfuses it, competes with it, until in the end the two are locked in a deadly contest, like the twin dominatrices of the Mother House religiosity, Afek, the creatress, and her archrival Boben, "who made all the journeys and performed all the miracles that Afek had done, but long afterward and only to claim credit for Afek's achievements." Self-destructive dialectic, like an extended parable of the cause-and-effect sequence that overdetermines our sense of reason or rationality, and that Wittgenstein called a "superstition."

Suppose Shakespeare's Prince Hamlet had the foreknowledge of all the actors who would follow him in acting out the sequence of the play. Suppose they would imitate the original so well or so poorly that every time the play were enacted a new Hamlet and a new Hamlet-problem would be born. Then Hamlet would not be Hamlet at all but Boben, "who made all the mistakes and bespoke all the soliloqueys that the real Hamlet had done," but only to claim credit from the original. But we do not in fact know what the original Hamlet had in mind, in large part because he changed his mind so often, and in that sense all the initiates in the *ban* system, plus their initiators, plus all the outsiders who come to investigate them, are Boben, for the real original will never be found, and if it were, it would have to be invented for the occasion, like Voltaire's God. Perhaps she is Barbara Jones (that would be my guess).

"A man goes to knowledge as he goes to war, wide-awake, with fear, with respect, and with absolute assurance" (Castaneda 1968: 32). In the sections that follow, I shall rely largely on Barth's fulsome descriptive account, and make use of the Pears and McGuinness translation of Wittgenstein's *Tractatus logico-philosophicus* (1961) to punctuate its empirical resonance with the *logos* of an indigenous New Guinea counterpart. I shall, however, merely adumbrate the significant details of Barth's account, and concentrate on its implications for the nautilus-spiral effect of obviation.

Laqsalman ban ("The child containment explanation")
Barth: chapter 4
Tractatus: 1. The world is all that is the case.

Conventional wisdom would suggest that the synthesis, the internal logic of the first three *ban*s with their common emphasis on inception, isolation, and the cognitive receptive naïveté of childhood would trace out the pattern of natural process: conception–gestation in the womb–childbirth, in that temporal order. But "conventional wisdom," often enough a tired euphemism for ingrained cause-and-effect thinking, would deny the impact of Barth's original hypothesis—largely correct as to the radical and counterintuitive nature of Ok epistemology—its deliberate obstruction of the causality assumptions.

Hence we should expect a direct inversion of the conventional (biological) inceptive monologue, something like childbirth–gestation–conception, and a corresponding subversion of the standardized metaphors for inceptive agency and cognition (the childbirth of thought and feeling), an ontological skepticism implicit in Barth's original argument. Since the publication of his first Ok book, many parallels have been found to this procedure—what John Keats called "negative capability"—elsewhere in Melanesia. A number of myths have been discovered by myself and others in which the temporal progress of the human lifecycle is reversed on itself: the character begins as an old person, "grows down" through the stages of life retroactively, eventually becoming an infant and disappearing into the womb. According to Thomas Maschio (1994), the Rauto people of New Britain regard metaphor itself as an infantile form of expression, and thereby reject what is commonly regarded as symbolism.

The very originality of origin is what is fêted in the *Laqsalman ban*. It is not the child itself, the neonate, the fetus, or the womb that is its object, but the afterbirth, the Boben of motherhood—the nurturing maternal succubus that is delivered after the child. (This may be a secret that the elders "keep from themselves" in the *ban*, but it is easily recovered from the context.) This is disguised in the central artifact of the *ban*, the *laqsal*, as the characteristic string-woven netbag in which mothers all over New Guinea carry their newly born infants—a portable, partible "second skin" that in this case ("The world is all that is the case") is worn, decorated with feathers, on the head of the *laqsal* novice and displayed in public. That, of course, is opposite to the fate of the (merely) physical afterbirth. It is important to emphasize this point in the full Wittgensteinian sense of the proposition: that the *laqsal* and all the rites and circumstances surrounding it (creation of a "second skin" for the initiate) is a made human artifact, crafted by the hands of the initiate's parents instead of the internal organs of the mother. But it is also vital to Barth's insight into the folly of interpretive symbolism up to that point, for the artifact, made of both "natural" and "cultural" substances, is (a) neither natural nor cultural, (b) neither adult nor infantile, and (c) neither symbolic nor real. This *ban*, as it were, "starts things going," and any species of anthropological interpretation that denies these facts denies the sanctity of the *ban* system.

Katiam ban ("The sacred relic-house explanation," colloq. "The smoking gun")
Barth: chapter 5
Tractatus: 2.1   We picture facts to ourselves.
              2.11 A picture represents a situation in logical space, the existence and non-existence of logical states of affairs.
              2.12 A picture is a model of reality.

The novices are "put down," subjected, with all the implications of an imprisoned, interiorized subjectivity (they might as well be postmodernists—minus the spiteful, passive-aggressive rhetoric). The second phase of obviational/initiatory (take your pick) synthesis trades on the metaphorical equation of house and womb found often in New Guinea (Daribi call them both by the same term, *be'*) and elsewhere in the world: medieval clerics in England used the Middle English term *husel*, "little house," for the *chi*, or human energy-aura. Although we have no direct evidence for Taoist concepts in the Mountain Ok, the *Katiam*, in which this *ban* is staged, is indeed a "little house." Officially, it is the sacred relic-house of the localized lineage (*kasel*) in which the tangible records of the ancestors and their activities are displayed, so that their powers, necessary for the growing of the staple crop taro, may be passively incorporated into the *sinik*, or soul-substance, of the initiate. It is a power-house of memories, one that remembers you back (note ergative usage), that in one sense resembles the Meso-American "recapitulation chamber" discussed in Castaneda—a crate or small enclosure in which the occupant attempts to reenact and rectify the salient memories of their life-course in order to obtain a Buddha-like enlightenment. What is wrong with this picture?

Plenty. For the *Katiam ban* registers the very opposite of recapitulative enlightenment, and would have to be called a precapitulation, since it reverses the order of the human life-course, and substitutes anticipatory intelligence (ancient

Greek Prometheus) for recollective intelligence (ancient Greek Epimetheus). This allows us to draw the following conclusions: in the *Katiam ban* the emphasis is on the cognitive reception of knowledge that will be valuable for the future rather than the active projection of a recovered past knowledge; the initiate in the *Katiam* is like a fetus in its mother's womb, whose perception is limited to nonverbal cues of its external environment; participation in the *Katiam ban* would have turned Carlos Castaneda inside out.

Hence point B in the obviation sequence, substituting the "case" of the womb for the afterbirth, is the cognitive and gestational midpoint in the synthesis, leading not from conception through containment to childbirth, but the reverse of that: from afterbirth through passive reception to childbirth and then conception. The arrow points the way.

Wunmalal ban ("The arrow demonstration")
Barth: chapter 6
Tractatus: 5.631   There is no such thing as the subject that thinks or entertains ideas.
          5.634   There is no a priori order of things.
          6.13   Logic is not a body of doctrine, but a mirror-image of the world.
William Shakespeare, *Henry V*: Blood is their argument.

Melanesians play hard ball; any suggestion of a sensitive or insensitive Freudian libido would be a profound misconception in this case, for anything even remotely resembling a "pleasure principle" would be bruised out of the initiate by the series of poundings (with stones), whipping, and beatings (with the painful stinging nettle) he receives on the skin, the body's most comprehensive organ of sensation. The would-be sensualist would be in need of kevlar, unheard of in these parts. In the case of the *Wunmalal*, the after-the-fact conception ("born screwed"), the programed emphasis is on inversive action—as in the "societies of contraries" found on the North American plains (who do everything backward)—and acute penetration as opposed to passive witnessing (as in the *Katiam*), in a sort of mute testimony to the copulatory act. The rite is held in the *Yolam* (the "Big House," as it were, called provocatively the "little sister" of the *Katiam*). "Is nothing sacred?" "Yes, as a matter of fact, it is." The treatment of the pig in preparation for the opening feast is a case in point, for it resembles closely the "reverse pig" technique used invariably by the Barok of New

Ireland on all public occasions (Wagner 1986). The Barok sequence goes like this: (a) the pig may not be purchased until it has already been killed, sealed in its sewn leaf-envelope, cooked to completion, and publicly displayed in that form; (b) the pig may not be put to death by any means other than suffocation; and (c) the pig may not be cut, divided, or portioned out until a whole series of rites, pronouncements, and taboos have been performed over it. (Picture in your mind a mass exodus of Mountain Ok people to New Ireland to see a pig feast done right; picture in your mind very few, if any, of them ever returning.)

The Faiwol sequence goes like this: (a) the pig is suffocated with a shoot from the black palm, a wood used normally in New Guinea for the making of bows; (b) "the fat from the flanks of this pig is then cut loose; it is heated in the fire and mixed with the black content from a dog's intestine . . .; this mixture is steam-cooked in leaves together with the dog's penis" (Barth 1975: 64); and (c) "the seniors grab bunches of nettles and whip the novices over the face and chest, causing great pain. They are then presented with the leaf package of the dog's black gut contents and cooked penis. They are forced to eat the mixture and at least lick and suck the penis" (Barth 1975: 65). German speakers might want to call this the *Schweinhundt ban*.

Humor, however, is not a part of the proceedings, though the *Wunmalal* has all the formal élan, fierce camaraderie, and inauthentic self-identification of a military hunting celebration held by torchlight somewhere in East Prussia. The most important thing is the pantomime of male childbirth enacted after the orgiastic main feast: "The novices are made to crawl on their hands and knees between the legs of the line of men; each man they pass under whips them with the burning nettles over back, legs, and particularly the genitalia" (Barth: 1975: 65). (Not only born screwed, but affectively all screwed up!) But is it really childbirth that is pantomimed here, or yet another painful simulation of copulation and conception? The sublimated canine oral penetration gives the answer, for it is not physical conception but mythical conceptualization (fictive fellatio) that is initiated here, for the active riposte to this passive oral reception is its oppositional figure–ground reversal transformation at point F, *Amkon ban*, when the initiates are first allowed to display their prowess in the telling of myths, foremost among them "The Myth of the Dog."

The *ban* system is initiatory in only one sense: that it is a staged progression, carefully regulated as to its content and enactment of cognitive awareness from passive and self-contained ignorance to full active participation in the design

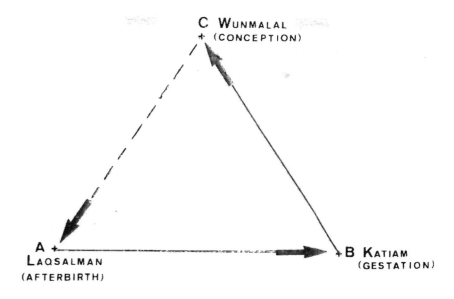

Synthesis: Retroactive conception

it superimposes on the course of human life. It does not merely "take on" a life of its own, it jump-starts one into being. Extreme exaggeration and hyperbole are necessary parts of this, so that the first three bans, *Laqsalman*, *Katiam*, and *Wunmalal*, form a Hegelian triad of thesis–antithesis–synthesis based on (1) the skin, the fact of containment itself as a "skin" or "house" enveloping and containing the subject; (2) impartial, naïve witnessing on the part of the subject, as an ethical precondition of its existence, being shown the mysteries instead of understanding them; and (3) penetrative containment dramatized through the simulation of being squeezed out in childbirth, being "drummed into" existence by whipping and pounding with stones and forced to lick or ingest loathsome substances and objects.

These three bans, via their internal logic and self-persuasive exercises, constitute together what is otherwise called the synthesis, the first half of the full obviation sequence. They are followed by three more, which take the form of encompassing, retroactive figure–ground reversals, and constitute together the antisynthesis: the *Mafomnang* (Telefol: *Mafuum-Ban*), the *Seban*, and the *Amkon*. These in turn develop an internal logic that basically incorporates the whole six-part obviation series of syntheses and antisyntheses, and are epitomized by a final, seventh stage that combines the passive and the active in a single expression of mutual and self-contradictory duality called the *Amowk*.

Mafomnang ban ("Pandanus mother explanation")
Barth: chapter 7
Tractatus: 4.121   Propositions cannot represent logical form: it is mirrored in them.
What finds its reflection in language, language cannot represent.
What expresses itself in language, we cannot express by means of language.
Propositions show the logical form of reality. They display it.
(This is the most transparent and self-paradoxical of all Wittgenstein's propositions, the virtual linchpin of the *Tractatus*. To say in so many words exactly what cannot be said in those very words is to show by meaningful example that language reflects its own inability to reflect and so on ad infinitum, like the infinite regression of mutual reflections that becomes apparent when two mirrors are placed face-to-face.)

The *Mafomnang ban* is the pivot-point of the whole series, a mirror-inversion of the procreative fantasy, initiating the sequence of three figure–ground reversal (D–A, E–B, and F–C) that requite, stage by stage, the temporal inversion consummated in the *Wunmalal* synthesis. In an apposite parallel to Proposition 4.121, it might be posed as the questions, "What reflects itself in the human life-cycle? How is the cognitive maturation of the individual reflected in the mysteries of symbolism, sexual receptivity, and gender interaction?" The obviation technology is uniquely depictive of this: self-understanding and the maturation process are modeled upon each other in the *ban* system, to the degree that each is a mirror-reflection of the other.

This is the display *ban* par excellence: in a marathon round of seclusion, feasting, carefully adorning the initiates, and carefully attending to the performance of their newly acquired ritual "skins" and headdresses, the display of the young men to themselves and to others takes the form of a "triumphant procession (Barth 1975: 74)—a kind of "cat's out of the bag/bag's out of the cat" ritualized revelation of what has become of the original placenta (D–A). The placentalized surrogate "mother" of the neonate reimaged in the new adult (cf. Wagner 2001: 234: "The one in the mirror borrows the action of looking to see itself"). The emergent pubescent male now wears the "bag" on his head, embellished by the tail feather of a hornbill, rather than presenting a birth-pouch to his mother, decorated with bird feathers. (This is significant: the male hornbill seals its mate in a hollow tree cavity so that she may incubate her young in safety, and feed them through an opening in the containment.)

The visual image of the standing panadanus tree, with its aerial roots so suggestive of lower limbs, and its tufts of dark, spikey leaves suggestive of elevated pubic hair, is iconic to the whole display. The ability of the pandanus tree to produce whole, living human beings from its husked fruiting pods, possibly as a figure–ground reversal of its symmetrically silhouetted human-pubic image, is a central feature of a great many Foi and Daribi myths, recorded by F. E. Williams, James F. Weiner, and myself. For these people its presence in the *ban* system would require no explanation. Nor would the "Tree of Life" motif, for a generalist like Joseph Campbell.

Hence the mirror-inversion motif is replete in its every detail—all the basic oppositions unified in a consummate image of upside-down symmetry: female/male, inside/outside, childhood/adulthood, isolation from mother/incorporation among the men of the *Yolam*, pubic hair/head hair, what can be represented in language/what language, instead, reflects.

Seban ban ("The high forest explanation")
Barth: chapter 8
Tractatus: 4.1212 What can be shown, cannot be said.
4.123 A property is internal if it is unthinkable that its object should not possess it.

For many of the interior New Guinea peoples, such as the Kaluli of Mt. Bosave, the house-roof as seen from within, and the crowns of the great rainforest trees as seen from above, are regarded as mirror-inversions of one another. They are in fact made of exactly the same leaves. Hence the figure–ground reversal enacted in this *ban*, which connects directly across the diagram with the passive containment of the initiates secluded in the *Katiam*, would have great significance for them. The substance of this *ban* is to requite the passive witnessing of the *Katiam ban* with an active male activity of going out into the high cloud forest to acquire and kill game animals: substitution—decontainment for containment;

remote hunting lodge for self-contained sacred relic house. (Cf. Wittgenstein: "A property is internal if it is unthinkable that its object should not possess it.") The game animals are prepared by the initiates and eventually taken down to the *Katiam*, where the food must be meticulously kept within the containment and eaten, and all refuse burned, so that none may be taken out of the house. As Barth notes: "Another major feature of Baktaman religion is made explicit, though perhaps no clearer in its implications, to the novices in the 5th degree initiation: the nature of secrecy, taboo, and 'true knowledge'" (1975: 81). The *Seban*, in Wittgensteinian terms or any other, is the self-evidencing of taboo.

Challenged by some Lutheran evangelists to find an equivalent term for "taboo" in their own language, the Daribi offered the term *habu*, and it was a penetrating insight. The *Seban* would seem to adapt or incorporate another feature characteristic of the Foi and Daribi peoples living in the limestone country south of the central highlands. This is the "crack between the worlds" tension between the young, celibate men secluded or sequestered in an impromptu hunting lodge, and the elders or older married men who represent the tradition of the settlement or "house" (*Katiam, Yolam*). This is discussed at length as the central theme of Foi poietics in Weiner's book *The empty place* (1991), and treated as the main focus of Daribi religiosity in my *Habu* (1973). The Mountain Ok *Seban* serves as a "go out there and fetch it" redress, a "Wittgenstein objective," to the passive witnessing of the second-degree initiates in the *Katiam ban*. In its turn it ushers in a reprieve from the forced seclusion of the *Katiam*, and a "degree of freedom" for the novices to explore the world of collective mythmaking represented by the *Yolam*.

Obviationwise, my students at the University of Virginia have developed a nickname for this particular turn (E–B) of the obviational screw: they call it "the twist of the knife in the gut."

Amkon ban ("The thatching the house-roof explanation")
Barth: chapter 9
Tractatus: 5.6   The limits of my language mean the limits of my world.
          5.621   The world and life are one.
          5.63   I am my world (the microcosm)

Quite possibly, in the counterintuitive way we have learned to think of these things, it was the *Seban*, the "twist of the knife in the gut," and not the topsy-turvy *Wunmalal* synthesis, that was the true original of the *ban* system. For just as the *Seban* connects across the pattern with the "little world" of the *Katiam* (E–B), so its successor the *Amkon* connects to the "big world" of the *Yolam*, the storytelling house that brings to life the collective, creative mythmaking that defines and identifies the true origins of the Mountain Ok world.

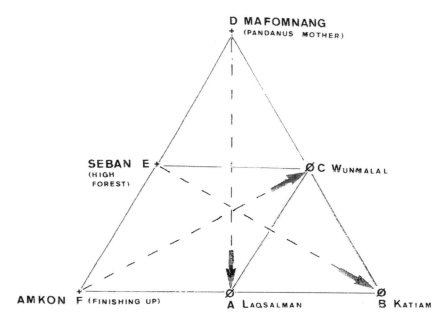

Antisynthesis: Proactive Mythmaking ("Creation")

It was Oswald Spengler, in the second volume of *The decline of the West* (1928), and not Wittgenstein, who brought the concept of "microcosm" into twentieth-century intellectual discourse. It corresponds to what I have called "the world in the person" as opposed to "the person in the world" of the macrocosm (Wagner 2001). The real danger implicit in the microcosm is not schizophrenia but solipsism (and Wittgenstein has written very eloquently on this). It is a worse peril than any of us could really imagine: not simply the claustrophobia of having twisted yourself into a little world of your own, but the rage on the part of the solipsist to find independent confirmation for the hermetically self-invented universe they have convinced themselves to occupy. What could an independent witness possibly tell them that would not seem the words of a ventriloquist's dummy? It is precisely this kind of confirmation that the *Amkon* offers to the self-secluded initiate, by collectivizing the preciously solipsistic "little world" in the exercise of mythic creativity—the storytelling realization of the exaggerated mythic origin of things.

This, too, deserves special comment: "Back in the beginning, stories sat around the campfire telling people to one another." Stories are shared people/people are individuated stories, and the nexus between them is the time-lapse of ancestry. This means that, like the "eternal logic of the Dreaming" of the Australian Aborigines, the temporal dimension of Afek, the creatress, was not simply a historical "past," but a wholly different epoch of reality, like the inside of a black hole, or a universe made of antimatter.

No surprise that this *ban* connects directly across the diagram to the "black dog" hunter's orgy of the *Wunmalal*, and performs the figure–ground reversal between the passive reception of myth and mythic agencies (such as the dog, as featured in the *Wunmalal*), and the assumption of active responsibility for those agencies on the part of the mature human being. As Barth remarks: "*Amkon* initiation is a large and complex ritual which combines many themes and is complicated by its elaboration of levels of audience segregation" (1975: 92). This amounts basically to the reintegration of the erstwhile novices into the full company of accomplished mature men ("made men," as the Mafia would have it) whose collective knowledge, necessarily mythical, of the Faiwol "big world" constitutes their macrocosm. Until that point the initiate was truly a "microcosm," living the mystery speculatively in what modern Americans would call "his own private Idaho."

Amowkan ("The Mother House explanation")
Barth: chapter 10
Tractatus: 6.54   My propositions serve as elucidations in the following way: anyone who understands me eventually recognizes them as nonsensical, when he has used them—as steps—to climb up beyond them. (He must, so to speak, throw away the ladder after he has climbed up it.)

Barth's explication is almost a word-perfect copy of Wittgenstein's: *Amowk* comes as the culmination of a long ladder of initiation, and gives the initiate status as a fully authorized senior. But in another sense, it is still only a stage in a man's religious education—only by repeated observation and increasingly responsible participation in rites does a man become an adept who feels at ease in the temples, at home with the idioms, and confident in his knowledge of the rites. In the words of one senior, "You know how it is during your initiation: your *finik* (spirit, consciousness) does not hear, you are afraid, you do not understand. Who can remember the acts and the words?" (Barth 1975: 101).

How much do they have in common, these two: one of the greatest ethnographers of all time, and the greatest epistemologist of the twentieth century? Wittgenstein, it is said, could whistle all of the symphonies of his namesake, Ludwig van Beethoven, from beginning to end, from memory, and Barth, at the end of his quest, could probably whistle the whole *ban* system exegesis in counterpoint with Beethoven's Ninth—"Tochter aus Elysium," etc. The *Amowkan* is the "third house," just as the *Katiam* was called "the little sister," and the *Yolam* the "big sister," so this one is the "mother" (as in "Mother House"). Taboos are relaxed, and for the first time in a sequence that has been monopolized by visual and tactile sensory emphases, the total acoustic makes its debut in the form of drums: drum knowledge, drum connotations, and drum design—a fitting consummation to a performance that has had as its focus the sounding of the human voice. (Though for Wittgenstein it would probably accord with the percussion sections marked *ritmo de tre battute* in the scherzo of Beethoven's Ninth—a wizardry of rhythmic elision and intensity that has been known to stun composers like Glinka and Verdi with awe.)

What Barth calls the seventh degree of initiation takes us beyond the counterpoise of con and gift that makes up the obviation cycle and brings us to the overview, the total picture, the point of release from narrative that Hegel called "Die Aufhebung" ("the uplifting"), and that Weiner calls "the sublation."

THE CHILD IN THE WOMB AND THE CORPSE IN THE GROUND

This statement, with its complete self-assurance and its point-on synchronization of the visual and the acoustic—its syntax of iconic tact (icon-tact, for short)—compresses the whole significance of the *ban* system into a single format. Yet it does not come from the Mountain Ok, but from the Barok people of central New Ireland, who have a very different perspective on life.

So why does it capture the sense of the Mother House initiation rite with such complete accuracy? Is it a coincidence that containment means exactly the same thing in both areas; that the expelling of the afterbirth precedes the act of conception in the Faiwol case, and the myth of origin supersedes biological reproduction? (Afek, the "Old Woman," actually created the ability to create.) For the Barok, as they explained it to me, the male role in the sexual act is to first conceive the woman's ability to conceive, and the male group leader, or Orong, is defined as being a temporally advanced gender inversion of the original, apical ancestress. Abstract, linear time drops out of the equation in both cases, and all we have left are the concrete images of gender inversion, containment, decontainment, and figure–ground reversal.

All of this would seem to add up to a set of classic structural permutations and combinations, tactfully iconic, of course. But in fact this is not so, for in both cases the structuralist assumptions are completely undermined by the epistemological imperatives that are taught along with them. The Mother House system shares with the Barok feasting complex a feature that is perhaps unique among initiatory programs, in that it accepts candidates on the basis of cognitive precocity alone, without regard to age-grade chronology. It is not there to "turn boys into men," like the Boy Scouts or most African and Native American initiations. All of these perform a normative function within society, like our own secondary schools. But neither "education" nor "socialization" is primarily what the *ban* system is all about. It is about nescience, the opposite of knowledge, as Jorgensen pointed out to me, and it is about antisociety, as Jones (1980) aptly demonstrated in her dissertation.

The real skill imparted to the initiates is for that reason very difficult to measure or second-guess, even with the remotest intentions in the world, though it lies at the core of all the secrecy attributed within the Mother House. It is like a mantra or a Zen koan that unites the point precision of the visual with the tactile resonance of the body's rhythms in a single flourish of embodied insight. And it is questionable how many initiates ever make it to that point.

But I am getting ahead of myself here. By the late 1970s the question of whether "society" even existed at all was on everybody's lips ("How can you measure a thing that isn't even there at all?")—it was anthropology's "dirty little secret." Barbara's discovery of what she called "consuming society" was something of a prodigy in its own right: a human aggregation that could only be what it pretended itself to be by breaking the rules for pretending, like Wittgenstein's Proposition 4.121. It was the first viable evidence for what Victor Turner called "antistructure" (and what I called, with his blessing, "obviation"). This is exactly why Barbara's Faiwol congeners told her that they were "cowboys": it was their job to safeguard the relics that ensure the growth of taro, the staple food. Without the relics, there is no taro, and without taro, there is no possibility of founding a community. But the very power that allows them to nurture life in their community also works insidiously against them, literally eats them alive from the inside out, forces them into the role of the ever-vigilant Western gunman. Like the so-called "drug problem" that afflicted First World nations at the time, it made Barbara's idiom of a self-consuming society more real than the conventional wisdom of the Establishment.

One of the implicit dangers in equating "information" with knowledge, as the internet generation has done, is that the quasi-hallucinatory effect of icon-tact is lost. How long does it take, in real time, for a social science to grow up? Secrecy of a most facile and unusual kind, perhaps "stealth secrecy," or secrecy made exponential by compounding it on itself, remains the enduring legacy of research in the Mountain Ok. This is already beyond the compass of common-sense social science "inquiry" strategies, and way beyond the cause-and-effect prevarication that Wittgenstein called a "superstition."

Not long after the completion of his initial research, Dan Jorgensen received an urgent message from the elders of the Mother House at Telefolip, requesting him to return and make a careful permanent record for posterity of everything connected with it—the lore, the stories, the procedures, and paraphernalia, etc.—because some jihad-crazed fundamentalist converts were threatening to burn the whole thing to the ground. Dan responded with his usual alacrity and resourcefulness, found funding (I received permission to divert some funding to him from my New Ireland grant), returned, and made the most impeccable recording possible under the circumstances. He made copies for himself, the elders, and the National Museum in Port Moresby, but when he returned to Telefolip some time later he discovered that the tapes he had left there had been recorded over by local youths with string band music. It was Vietnam all over again!

MAKING CONTACT WITH THE MOTHER HOUSE

Here is how things stood as of June 2000:

1. I had spent the better part of my career in awe of the Mother House and its premier researchers: Fredrik Barth, Barbara Jones, and Dan Jorgensen.

I had never even set foot (not an easy thing to do thereabouts) in the Star Mountains region.

2. I had trained Barbara in the essentials of New Guinea fieldwork at Northwestern University, before I was "persuaded" (with major prejudice) to depart that once-proud institution. We remained in touch during her time at Imigabip; when she returned she found there was no one on the faculty at Northwestern (this, by the way, is an understatement) qualified to supervise the writing of her dissertation. Very generously, my new colleagues at Virginia voted to accept her into our graduate program, and Barbara and I took it from there.

3. Barbara's dissertation, "Consuming society," provides the most convincing documentation of a negative sociality in the ethnological record. I think both George Orwell and Philip K. Dick would stand in awe of it, and Oswald Spengler would throw in the towel.

4. Joel Robbins, Virginia's second prodigy researcher into the Mountain Ok region, was hard at work on his masterpiece about Christian fundamentalist conversion among the Urapmin, *Becoming sinners* (2004), a work that would upstage (annihilate would be the better word) Bercovitch's "curse of the Mountain Ok."

5. Earlier that spring Virginia's third prodigy researcher into the Mountain Ok, Michael Wesch, had made arrangements for me to accompany him on a fact-finding mission to the Mother House complex at Telefolip—the "Vatican," so to speak, of the whole operation. This was pursuant to Mike's search for a field site of his own.

This is a good place to start, for the site that Mike eventually selected, Tumobil, a community straddling the boundary with West Papua, was the second of the original Mother Houses established by Afek, the creatress. According to our informants, they were, in order:

1. Telefolip;
2. Bantavelobip (Tumobil);
3. Bultem (site of the artificial mining town Tabubil);
4. Imingabip (e.g., "Imigabip"), site of Barbara Jones's research.

Dan Jorgensen told me that Afek had also created another house at Oksapmin, to the east, and "put all the colors in the world in it." Unfortunately, as the story goes, the different colors, being so diverse, cannot abide one another, and so they clashed, and the house exploded, and the colors flew out and settled onto everything (and that, the people say, is why things have their different colors). Afek, all unbeknownst to herself, had invented the Doppler effect, the "red shift" later discovered by astrophysicists.

In short, Afek (Faiwol: Afekan, Karigan) was a prodigy creatress indeed! Her "thing" was originality, a scarce commodity in anthropology, and the original world she created, they say, was overfull of unbelievably beautiful, fragile things—things that because of their own inherent beauty and perfection cannot last, and their inherent obviation or self-destruction triggered the beginning of *biniman* (Jorgensen's "entropy"), the eventual coming apart of everything that will lead to the end of the world.

What we have here, in mythic time, is an immense stretch of highland topography transected at all possible angles by convergent and divergent story lines masked as creative journeyings, a world map of miracles reminiscent of nothing so much as the Traveling Creator songlines of aboriginal Australia. What we have in real time is an immense paradigm of information overload, of the kind dreaded by librarians, bureaucrats, and computer specialists, a self-repleting echo chamber of objectified memories and details that recalls Borges's story about an Argentinian named Funes whose memory-process elaborated on its details rather than simplifying them. It is virtually impossible to follow a Mountain Ok narrative at any length without being subdivided fractalwise into alternative story lines and cues for other scenarios. (This is one of those mythologies in which the main problem is not that of putting stories together but of keeping them apart.) Memory is key, and topography is key.

"This whole ground is made out of stories," said M., the ingenious young Telefol intellectual whom Mike had arranged to be our interpreter and guide, "there are five or six big ones about Afek, and eight or nine little ones. Even these little mounds of earth [indicating with his hands] have stories attached to them." One of the most remarkable features of these stories, besides their déjà vu-like play of almost-identical plot devices and outlines shuffling between them, is that the identities of men and places tend to be relatively fixed and stable, whereas those of the women are remarkably deceptive, duplicitous, and mercurial—suggestive of parallactic displacement, obverse twinning, bipolarity, mood-swings, shape-shifting, and worse. We shall see presently that this has profound implications for what could be called the "outcome epistemology" of the Mother House ("La donna è mobile").

Pilgrimage

Proceeding in company with Mike and M. on a fine day, we walked from the
rest house at Telefolmin station to the ancient site of the Telefolip. At a fork
in the road as we neared the spot was a sort of faux neo-Christian dummy
replicate, perhaps a "Becoming Sinners Theme Park," constructed by a radical fundamentalist organization off to the left, whereas to the right the road
wound along some of the iconic power imagery made famous in Ok lore. On
the left we passed a compound of recently built "traditional" houses, and then
on the right the religiously preserved house-site of Dan Jorgensen. Immediately after that on the right was the original grove of pandanus trees—the
first ones in the world and "the root of all food" created by Afek—and then,
proceeding downhill, after some turns in the road, we came to the sacred
ground, divided according to strict protocols (as often among the Australian
Aborigines into men's and women's "country," and protected, according to M.,
by strong taboos).

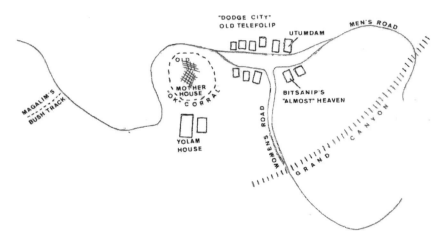

Telefolip—A "Western" perspective

I made terse notes following the explicatory glosses provided by M. as we
toured the site, and also drew a rough sketch map, reproduced here, using a self-
consciously "Western" nomenclature that might prove endearing to Barbara,
whose ancestor had been an American cavalry officer ("Afek's Last Stand").
There, inside a corral-like fence were the ruins of the great old Mother House,
partly covered by a blue tarp, and looming over it was the high, gaunt *Yolam*

house, a "multi-storied" affair, and next to it perhaps the *Katiam*, incubating the world's images within. Here we have the secret of Afek's purely anticipatory creativity, not immoral at all but in fact totally amoral, for it turns out that Afek was an incarnation of pure intention: she was entirely unable to think (e.g., reflect), but could only act. ("Nothing either good or bad," as Hamlet points out, "but thinking makes it so.") Here I shall refer directly to my notes, made on the occasion:

When Afek built the spirit house she killed two people to "open" it. A Tifalmin boy of eleven–thirteen she killed; the second was a person from Feranmin. She opened the house using blood. She cut the bodies, and rubbed the blood in the posts around the fireplace. She built the house on top of a man who tried to "play" with her, and that was the Telefolip. The bones and substance are still there; there are two or three more important things inside. The main entrance is the deepest hole in the southern hemisphere.

This particular "Dodge City" even had a "post" office; one of the houses has a very peculiar posthole underneath it, to which M. refers as "the gateway to hell" (aren't they all?). When the post decays, they will rebuild the whole building on the spot. Then they insert the new post, and they will not have to shove it, it will go into the ground by itself. Millions and millions of flies and maggots inside, very hot inside. Area where the post is located is called _____ (I did not get the name, possibly something like "The Federal Building," or some unreasonable facsimile thereof).

Even had a census bureau (more likely noncensus bureau). Last house on left side of Old Telefolip row, M.'s brother said this house is significant. If you take off the cover of the house-board, you will find a carbon-like black object, like battery-acid. This thing will melt and melt, and when it melts completely there will be no more people. Now it is very small. *Utumdam*: "When this is finished, the people will turn to stone (*tum*)." It is a tube; every year it is reduced by some millimeters. M. believes this will indicate some major changes (demographics? global warming? carbon emissions?).

Eleven houses in all, both sides of the street, like a very much weathered western movie set, complete with cowboys and gamblers. City on the dodge. Lawbreakers, jawbreakers, etc. Outpost/inpost. Hard-packed clay (laterite) platforms reaching up toward the floor inside the wooden posts that hold up the house. This represents the ages of the houses built on that spot for they mark the height where the ground level was when they were first erected there (four hundred years, according to Pam Swadling).

Coming toward the end of Main Street, we reached a turning point, one of the most significant "double woman" episodes in the quest for the real Barbara Jones. There, standing by the roadside, as though by pure happenstance, was a singularly poised and beautiful young woman, bearing (actually flashing) the long, straight nose that is the hallmark of erotic beauty for all Papua New Guinea.

I was shown a youngish woman in the small group of line houses in the complex on the other side of the (male/female) separation, and was told she was the "king . . . no, the queen" of the Telefolip. I asked if she had not taken the place of "the Old Woman," and was told "yes." I suggested that she might be a reincarnation of Afek, citing the example of the Dalai Lama, and was told "possibly, but we are not sure."

Field notes are necessarily cryptic, but the actual exchange that took place on this occasion was far more interesting. It had occurred to me as I was being presented to Her Majesty that these people might have only a very sketchy idea of what "reincarnation" means, so I took M. aside and explained the concept in detail. Then I asked, "Is this woman, the queen of the Telefolip, the reincarnation of Afek?" His answer, "Almost . . . but not quite," told me more than I wanted to know, but it put a whole new spin on things. What it means, literally, is that because of *biniman*, the deterioration or running down in time that is in the nature of things, every time a new "Afek" is born her powers will be somewhat less than those of the one who came before her. What it means figuratively, in terms of the situation that presented itself at that moment, is that here is a new generation of educated Telefol that is willing to talk in scientific prose if need be, and share insights with outsiders such as myself. This gave me a kind of parallactic perspective on the role of the queen, whose name, I learned, is Bitsanip.

When you die, you come to a junction; the first road, Kabuntigin, leads down to the Sepik River (of course!); the second road, Agabel, leads southwest to the Western Province. On the first road is the "person" or *masalai* ("place spirit") Kabuntigin-Kiak, who eats the flesh of the dead, leaving the bones. Fengfengbel ("Devours the Flesh") is the road that leads to hell—"tearing the meat hell" (and, unless I miss my guess, crocodiles & Margaret Mead as well!). The second road leads to heaven; nothing will meet you, you will have no trouble. The queen is the owner of the house that includes the gate to heaven (marked "Bitsanip's 'Almost' Heaven" on the Dodge map); when a person died in the old days the queen would "direct" them to the good road. A man from Urapmin found a "sealed" road inside a cave ("big enough for two cars") that goes to Bultem, leads up to Telefolip, and ends up at the "gate" of the queen. Because of the road, aid is being given to the people.

I was told that an alternative name for the bad road is "The Road of Dogs Tearing Flesh," and this puts me in mind of something I was told by the distinguished Mexican archaeologist Dr. Lopez-Lujan as he guided me through the excavations beneath the ancient Aztec Templo Mayor in the heart of Mexico City (Tenochtitlan). He said that the Aztecs believed that the newly deceased, upon entering the road to the Underworld (Mayan Xibalba), would be met by a powerful dog, who would shield and protect them from the horrendous demons waiting to attack them if they had been kind to dogs during their lifetime, but leave them to the mercy of the demons if they had not. (Shades of the Roman Cerberus!)

MEET ... GONDORFF

The term "grifter" is American underworld slang for the type of con artist who preys upon other con artists—often to the point where the very finesse involved in doing so becomes its own reward, as depicted in the masterful Hollywood film epic called *The sting*. Mike and I had an appointment the next day with the man I am calling "Gondorff" here, after the Chicago grifter played by Paul Newman in that movie. He was one of the senior elders of the old Mother House, and one of Dan Jorgensen's informants, though I never did catch his name. Normally we would not get a chance to see someone in that class, but Mike had prevaricated just a little and told him that I had been Dan's teacher, though it was really the other way around.

What followed on that occasion, in fact the whole trip, was neither traditional nor contemporary, and neither part of the big world of "global" modern world civilization nor of the small world of postcolonial emulation, but one of those parallactic double visions that allows one to see through the whole charade, just like the concluding scene in *The sting*. It also bore more than a passing resemblance to the Emerald City of Oz: "We're not in Kansas anymore."

In any event, we entered one of those upstanding, foursquare traditional Telefol houses next day, with its twin hearths: The Taro hearth, or hearth of nurturance, and the Arrow Hearth, or hearth of killing. I had asked our host to tell us one of those "five or six big stories about Afek," and so it began (at least this is as much as I can decipher from my notes: I actually drew a kinship diagram):

Telefolip has five (patri)clans. First clan: Unap married two women, first a good wife and then a bad wife. The bad wife was either named or was from Nagaramkel (Ningeramtem, down below on the Sepik River); the good wife was either named or was from (it may not matter) Tem Talip. Upon the good wife Unap fathered two sons, Ninai and Yayap, in that order, and upon the bad wife he also fathered two, Bafanim and Unsigim, in that order. Unap and Ninai went along the River Sol to find meat and pandanus. They met the devil(?), and brought the population to Telefolmin. Atemkiakmin was the lineage of Utem Ninai, later gave rise to many peoples. Bafanim and Unsigim, using half a plank, cut apart the two-headed man of Feranmin at a place called Igantil. Then they died.

(Note-taking of this sort is notoriously difficult in Papua New Guinea, and I had had plenty of experience at Karimui and New Ireland. What is left unsaid or is carried by pure innuendo holds the whole meaningful or metaphoric value of the narrative, and the place- and person-identities, when decipherable at all, simply serve as points of reference.)

Three of the clans died out; now they had only two. They made a bridge over the River Om at Oksapmin, lived in a cave, came up, crossed the Sepik, and came to Eliptamin. They came up to the mountain Atingbil north of Telefolmin, brought pigs and marsupials to the place (apparently for the first time). The string bag broke, let loose pigs and marsupials at the River Fula, and these were the ancestors of all the pigs and marsupials in the area. Went to urinate, urine came up white(?). (Apparently the subject is female from this point.) Crossed the River Sepik at Faliktum, made a bridge, went to Urapmin. All the (species of) insects and snakes "they saw this woman coming and they left," the bridge broke and they went inside the water. Afek went to the side, Urapmin, she killed a man, then brought him back—"Satan," a very bad man (e.g., the man who had followed the River Sepik. Boben was the Old Woman, the "queen." She made Bultem on the River Tem; her younger sister Didiben, the queen's younger sister, her child had grille, skin diseases, gave rise to the line of Ningerum. The older sister, Boben, created Telefolip, created Bultem, came back to the origin place. The little grandmothers together they originated Bultem. Telefolip started started fighting with Bultem, made an agreement or alliance. She straightened the road, went to Bultem, came back via Imigabip. Boben made this road, followed the road of Afek, brought population. Boben wanted to claim credit for the work of Afek; she bad-mouthed Afek, "It was me, it was me alone!"

Now it becomes clear what is going on here. The "story," as it were, has no beginning and no end, but is made up of constant interruptions of itself, in the manner of Tony Crook's "changing the subject in mid-sentence," a psychological ploy to delude both storyteller and audience alike into imagining that it might be either one story or many stories, and to maintain the suspension of disbelief as to secrets revealed and secrets withheld. Gondorff indeed, get my grift? The "history" as well as the "structure" of the narrative were not readily distinguishable as such, for the real motivator of the story is the space/time dyslexia or "temporal reflex sorcery" that serves as the raison d'être for the whole ban system.

Boben went to Urapmin, met all the snakes and insects; if the bad man had not met her, she would have caused people to shed their skins when they get old, but now it is just the snakes and insects that can do so. Koimtiginkiak, he saw the road to hell, the Sepik road. He followed Boben, slipped on the bridge, fell in the river. Boben was making new skins for the snakes and insects but Koimtigin (Sinapugtigin) raped her, and she did not make such skins for people (thereby dooming them to mortality).

At this point in the narrative (or whatever) I found myself quite literally floored. I had found myself in this place many, many times before in the field, and began experiencing more or less cumulative déjà vus—the dear old fragrance of woodsmoke, the smoke-stained trophy pig's jaws stuck into the woven walls and roof, the same episodes repeated over and over with different contexts and characters each time, the real or studied ambiguity of pronominal reference that makes it almost impossible to tell who is doing what and with what and to whom. So I put up my hand and signaled the narrator to stop: "Wait a moment; I'm confused here; just who was it that was making a skin by the bridge when she was raped? Was it Afek, or Boben?"

"*That's it,*" he shouted, "*you got it!*"

Déjà vu was the whole story all along: game, set, and match. The correct answer was not "Afek," "Boben," "Didiben," or "the queen," but *whether* Afek, Boben, Didiben, or the queen, and has nothing to do with shape-shifting at all. It has to do with a diabolically clever and chiasmatic manipulation between intention and memory that is found in (a) the writings of Carlos Castaneda, (b) the sting engineered by Gondorff in the movie of that name, (c) most forms of sleight-of-hand magic, (d) the political agendas of late Roman Emperors like Caligula and Nero, (e) most forms of secretive killing sorcery used in highland New Guinea, and (f) a self-paradoxical evocation of the duality principle called "The Two Dolls," which serves as the outcome epistemology of the Mother House.

CALIGULITY: THE NATURAL AND PREDICTABLE RESULT

Mike Wesch and Joel Robbins had told me stories of the modeled heads of Western mass-marketed baby dolls showing up in the reliquaries of various peoples in the Mountain Ok region. (Imagine the panic that would ensue if some product designer came up with a Boben-Barbie!) Perhaps these gratuitous finds lent a myth to the ideology that surfaced in my ongoing conversation with Gondorff, the elder, but the epistemology is something that belongs to the Mother House alone:

> You see them hovering over mountain peaks at night, like UFOs. One of us saw one spinning above the whirlpool you passed by on the way over here. The route of the dolls is that they go from mountain to mountain. Dolls, gold (probably a reference to the gold mine at Ok Tedi), everything is the heritage of the Old Woman. She got a knife made of nipa pine, built a house on top. In the middle they will build a house, take two dolls, allow people from the US to take a look.
>
> The dolls are not like stones; they are like glass and very shiny, if you look directly at them you will be blinded. People cannot look directly at them. The dolls move at night from mountain to mountain, they follow the footsteps of Afek and her three sisters; they follow the footsteps of the Old Woman.
>
> Fontamnok is the father of the man who looks after the two dolls; he asked the key people from outside if they could come in and take a closer look. A large multinational corporation wants to buy them, but they will not be available until the man who presently owns them dies. They are worth 27 billion, no (correcting himself) 27 trillion Kina.

Like twin Barbie-dolls each trying desperately to out-Barbie the other? Not exactly—these are something rich and strange, very rich and very strange. The conception of these dolls, in other words, is opposite to the way in which we ordinarily think of dolls: they are subjects that behave like objects rather than objects that behave like subjects: inside-out Barbies, so to speak.

The Two Dolls are the natural and predictable outcome of the obviational process that began with the inversion of the human life-course at the very inception of the *ban* system: the "afterbirth" of the *Laqsalman ban*. A self-anticipating sequence is set up: what began as an effort to control something that is normally outside of human control ends up by controlling one. On the behavior front, this can be intuited as the Caligula effect, or the "behavior of the weak": deliberately breaking rules so as to call attention to oneself. (Both Caligula and Nero were basically weak personalities in terms of self-esteem, and had to rely on role playing in order to acquire enough stage presence to rule the empire.)

One sets up a course of action in which a surprising outcome is already anticipated in the steps that come before it, creates a self-modeling sequence of events that has nothing to do with the cause-and-effect sequence. A direct analogue can be found mathematically in the Fibonacci sequence: each subsequent member of the series equals the sum of the previous two, so that the "Two Dolls" reiterate themselves automatically with the appearance of each third term— both reflecting themselves in their antecedence and foreshadowing themselves in their precedence.

Here we have another point of resonance between the Mountain Ok peoples and the Daribi. Both have a mathematical system based on threes: in the Mountain Ok case increase is done exponentially, by powers: 3^1-3^2-3^3, so that the ultimate number is the ultimate number (*biniman*, the end of the world, will come with the twenty-seventh rebuilding of the Mother House). In the Daribi case the key is division rather than multiplication: there are only three recognized numbers, so that the Two Dolls reintegrate themselves in the curious form of duality that serves as the balancing point of number, called *sidari-si*, literally "the two-together two."

The secret of Afek's creativity—what she did at the very beginning—is a self-implicating form of *biniman*: she broke all the rules before they came into being, like some mythical travesty of the "big bang" theory. So that all we have left is the afterbirth of her "original sin" in the form of an entropic end result, a concept of order that gradually decays as the world-process works toward its natural conclusion.

CHAPTER 4

The ontology of representation

ENTELECHY: THE SELF-MODELING OF THE EVENT HORIZON

At the most basic level of human experience lies the happening of events. Just as we do not really know what an event or happening really is, in the sense of defining it properly, so we do not know why or how events happen in whatever particular order, or indeed lack of order, that we may ascribe to them. There has never been, nor will there ever be, a science of events, still less an art, given the fact that what we call "chaos" is simply the most recondite order of all. Thus we are brought face to face with the specter of nonlinear causality, and at the same time with both self-modeling and the subject/object shift, or in other words the integral reciprocity of ends and means.

Space, as we normally understand it, is only a picture of itself. What we call "space" in the simplest and most elemental sense is only a picture of itself; it is not the real thing. Three-dimensional length, breadth, and depth exists only in the picture-space of the human imagination, and exists outside of it, "out there in the world," only by projection. This concept of artificial space as an objectified reality corresponds exactly to what the philosopher Gottfried Wilhelm Leibniz ([1714] 1989) called the monad. That is, space, which we naturally objectify in the act of perception, is a self-modeling phenomenon, an isometric scale model of the codependency of the three dimensions. Hence the picturing of three-dimensional space, a human and not a natural construct, is a self-modeling—a direct self-imitation—of the mutual codependency of the three dimensions. This is modeled isometrically in the obviation diagram, which likewise depends upon three major axes (Illustration C of Dimensional co-dependency, below).

Just as three-dimensional space is a picture of itself, so the action of obviation is a picture of itself—it literally depicts, in the form of motion rather than stasis, the codependency of the three dimensions on one another. But there is a big difference between a moving and a static depiction of the same thing. A static picture represents its subject only in terms of basic form, whereas a moving picture (as in the cinema) represents its subject in terms of events or happenings (thus the film *Casablanca* represents an event rather than a simple geographical locus). What makes obviation special is that the events it depicts can be seen as happening one after another, in a time-sensitive or temporal sequence, or else as all happening at once—a metaphor spread out, with all the times in one space. In the latter case, to paraphrase Victor Zuckerkandl, obviation takes place "in a dimension perpendicular to time" (1973: 191).

What does this mean? It means that the third-point perspective necessary to the full representation of obviational motion has an event structure all its own, that the one you see in the mirror has borrowed the action of looking to see itself, that the phenomenon of mirror-reflection actually transposes events into a retrograde version of themselves. It turns picturing into unpicturing. This imitates the effect of what I have called the "mirror wheel," a wheel that revolves in three dimensions instead of only two, and thus literally turns out of the space of its own self-depiction. On this basis, the action of obviation itself, with the compounded revolution of each of the three axes into an opposite dimensional configuration to the one it had had before, is that of unpicturing its prior existential (ontological) status. It is out of its own picture of itself, having obviated the picture space necessary to its own happening as such, and thus also uneventuated itself. In other words, what is generated by the action of obviation is the isometric equivalent of the event horizon generated by retrograde gravitic activity in the interior of a black hole. Space, the only place in which events can happen, is *unpictured as it passes through the event horizon, and therefore the events themselves cease to exist.* This gives a new meaning to "obviation."

What we have learned from the "black hole" analogy is that "event" and "energy" are two different words for the same thing: the cosmos models itself upon itself. The conceptual problem here is that what we know of as "energy" is completely invisible and undetectable except where it is in transition from one

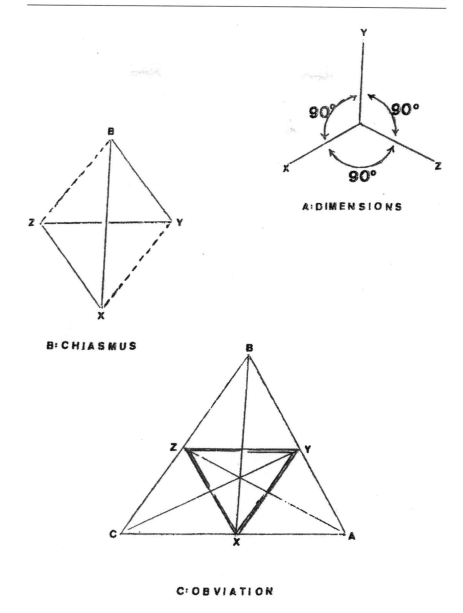

Dimensional co-dependency

"kind" or "state" of energy to another. That is, there is no such thing as "energy in and of itself," or "energy in being," but only energy as a becoming transformation from one objectifiable form of it to another: a star only becomes a star when

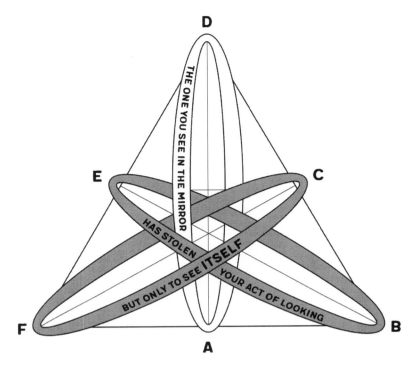

Third point perspective

the optic nerve turns the photonic energy of its emission source into neuronic energy.

"But," you object, "if there is no such thing as a stable, definable form of energy, how can we speak of a transition between two such states?" Good point, for it leads us back to the question of metaphor and the modeling of analogy upon analogy, as in the double-proportional comparison and ultimately obviation. In other words, if "visible light" is a metaphor combining wavelength and the electromagnetic spectrum, it can only be represented as such by virtue of another analogy (as above) combining the photonic emissions entering the eye and their transforming into neural energy via the optic nerve.

But if stars only become real stars when transformed by the neuronic event-energy of the brain-body complex, how can we speak of the cosmos itself as a self-modeling reality, and what is meant by holography in this context?

Leibniz called the agentive (proactive) aspect of this entelechy, drawing upon the Greek roots for "being" (*ent*) and "communication" (*tele*), implying that the self-isolating monads, or atomic fields of consciousness, that make up reality are in unwitting communication with one another by virtue of their absolute identity of form as holographic entities. In other words entelechy is a form of resonance implicit in the fact that individual monads vibrate in synchronic rapport with one another just as individual components of a crystal all resonate on the same frequency. Because of this, intrinsic, part/whole resonance is as much a property of the self-modeling of monads (consciousness) as it is of holography.

CHIASMATIC COSMOLOGY: THE NATURAL HISTORY OF THE EVENT HORIZON

It is known that Albert Einstein acknowledged the possibility of the black hole. Had he paid more attention to his colleague Kurt Gödel, who, we are told, would lecture him on the shortcomings of relativity theory, he would have done more than admit it—he would have proven it. For as Gödel must have noticed, Einstein's famous field equation $E = mc^2$ is a quadratic equation, and a quadratic equation, by definition, necessarily has two roots, a positive one and a negative one. This means, of course, that the velocity of light, represented by c (for "celerity") in the equation, must necessarily admit of both negative and positive valuations.

Every quadratic equation is an instance of the double-proportional comparison that defines chiasmatic logic, which is the definitive metric of Gödel's Proof. But what is a negative velocity, and how would electromagnetic emission, subject to such a qualification, behave? Instead of expanding outward, like the ripples from a stone thrown into a pond, negative light would spin inward, like water going down a drain, or like the accretion disc of a black hole. In other words, whereas the net effect of light's positive velocity would be an expanding universe (I am indebted to E. A. Milne for this insight), that of a negative velocity (thanks, Kurt!) would be a centripetal vortex, accretion disc, event horizon, and all.

THE ONTOLOGY OF REPRESENTATION

The act of representation, the most naïve, primitive, and even childlike of all the traits that make us human, is not a fait accompli of the imagination. It is not meaningful, as they say, or significative in and of itself. It is an act of miniaturization, in the way that the metaphor or trope not only miniaturizes language, but literally turns it inside out, denies the thing it represents by representing the thing it denies. Hence the metaphor represents by means of a double-proportional comparison of the symbol with the symbolized, the thing that it stands for.

We are indebted to the poet J. W. von Goethe for the observation that "telescopes and microscopes magnify the insignificant." It is impossible to understand what miniaturization really means unless one is caught up in its image. Otherwise one is faced with the difficult problem of deciding whether magnification actually makes the thing one is observing larger and the observer smaller, or vice versa. And it is not a trivial issue, either, for there is nothing in the universe that suggests that reduction in scale has anything to do with the starry heavens. It is our problem, we conveniently assume, but since we are also a part of the universe we are observing, it is also the universe's.

Scale-change is no less a chiasmatic phenomenon than time and space, and one of the foundational attributes of representation. It is based on a double-proportional comparison between the model and the thing represented in it; between the scale and the model, such that the scale of the model is the model of the scale, or in other words the representation of reality is the reality of the representation.

It was Claude Lévi-Strauss (1966), in his discussion of the science of the concrete, who first called attention to the importance of the miniature small-scale model: the illusion more real than the thing itself. The text is worth quoting in its entirety:

> What is the virtue of reduction either of scale or in the number of properties? It seems to result from a sort of reversal in the process of understanding. To understand a real object in its totality we always overcome by dividing it. Reduction in scale reverses this situation. Being smaller, the object as a whole seems less formidable. By being quantitatively diminished, it seems to us qualitatively simplified. More exactly, this quantitative transposition extends and diversifies our power over a homologue of the thing, and by means of it the latter can be grasped, assessed, and apprehended at a glance. A child's doll is no longer an enemy, a rival, or even and interlocutor. In it and through it a person is made into a subject. (Lévi-Strauss 1966: 23)

Lévi-Strauss's brilliant insight effectively establishes the balance between scale-change and scale-retention as a self-imitative principle in its own right: a diagnostic criterion for the understanding of cultural imagery via the conscious-ness that supports it, a kind of self-imitative symmetry of the subject/object shift.

Why call this a symmetry? Because each "side" of the double image places the other in a perspective that is inverted to its own, a reciprocal engagement of viewpoints. Hence the ontology of representation itself became a focal point for the development of human sentience, first identifiable in the cave art of the later Paleolithic era. What does it mean that the artists silhouetted their own hands on the rock wall by spraying pigment around them? The human hand is the signature image here, subject and object at once; both the agency of the representation and the thing represented in it.

The representation of the glacial-era fauna (Villefranchian) in the ancient Iberian rock art "keeps the scale," so to speak, of the self-agentive drawing hand, captures the habitus, the "pride of movement" or *zhac*, as the Athabascan shamans of Canada call it, of the creatures depicted simultaneously with their specific body-shapes—creates a Picasso-like dramatization of body-in-motion and motion-in-the-body. I once asked an expert on the ancient cave paintings for her own take on this primordial fantasy of motion-in-being and being-in-motion, and what it might have meant to the original artists themselves. She replied that we have lost the oral tradition of those who make the Iberian paintings—too much time and too much history had intervened between then and now. Fortunately, she added, some observers in South Africa had been able to interview participants in the Kalahari cave painting tradition in about 1850. What the indigenous artists told them was that they had thought that if they could represent the creatures with true-to-life accuracy and spirit, their real-life counterparts would appear automatically in the space just outside the cave.

Examples like this would suggest that visual representation is in itself an effect of miniaturization. Most of the things seen by the eye are larger than the eye itself, and the eye itself, as Wittgenstein observes, is never within its own field of vision. Even when one looks in a mirror, for example, what one perceives is a back-to-front laterally inverted miniaturization of the organ that is trying to look at itself. The eye cannot see itself seeing itself. But for the Barok people of New Ireland, those experts on the reciprocity of perspectives, the eye's mode of vision is not unidirectional, but parallactic. "Here" and "there" are merged into a single point of focus, a "here and here," as in a surveyor's par-allactic baseline. Their conception of "the eye" is very different from our own: it represents itself within the thing it sees, and the thing it sees within itself, like a double-proportional comparison between the eye itself and the object of its vision. Hence the Barok word for "eye," *mara*, is chiasmatic in its intent: it means the perfect identity formed between the point of focus within the eye and the object of that focus in the world around it. (This seems to be reflected in the Barok "good luck" blessing: *lak mamaran*, literally "luck in the double focus.") The eye sees itself seeing itself in this double take on our own nonchiasmatic assumption: Barok do not simply see the world, they survey it.

What does it mean to imitate oneself imitating oneself? Is the reciprocity of perspectives observable on a behavioral scale as well? The best evidence we have comes from the Malaysian *latah* syndrome, a behavioral pattern of self-imitation more commonly known as "imitative hysteria." It is a prime example of cognitive autoreaction, a neuronic feedback loop dysfunction that has its origin in the perfect identity formed within the mind between the motor impulse to act in a certain way and the homologue of that impulse discovered in the world around one. In other words the *latah* syndrome is the behavioral equivalent of the Barok concept of vision.

In the classic case, *latah* begins with a startle reaction: the victim is startled by a flashing light or loud noise and moves immediately to check their spasmodic reaction, but since that spasmodic reaction is identified immediately with the thing that caused it, the victim winds up imitating the gestures they go through in their own efforts to banish it: acting out the behavior one is trying to avoid as a necessary part of avoiding it. The action becomes commutative as witnesses take their self-imitational cues from the others they can observe around them, and begin to imitate others' self-imitations of themselves. Thus it is important to understand that the action is involuntary but perfectly conscious, so that the victims are well aware of what they are doing, but also of the fact that they have no means to stop it, since trying to stop it is precisely the thing that keeps it going.

The analogy of *latah* to laughter is a hard one to miss: both are initiated by a startle reaction—an incongruous event or a joke in the case of laughter—and both are sustained by the impulse to check them, such that the impulse to check eventually takes the place of the joke itself. (Professional comedians, like the late Jack Benny, often use this self-imitative effect as a technique to send their audiences into a self-imitative hysteria of laughing at their own attempts to stop themselves from laughing that is in no way differentiable from *latah*.)

For that matter, it is also hard to overlook the analogy with sexual orgasm, which is likewise, in case you haven't noticed, set into action by the impulse to check it, resulting in an imitation of one's own self-imitation that sometimes leads to the formation of a small-scale miniature model of the human body called an "embryo." As an example of self-representation, in this case of the human race itself, this recalls the testimony of the Kalahari cave artists, that if they could represent the creatures with true-to-life accuracy and spirit, their real-life counterparts would appear automatically in the space just outside the cave.

Just what, in any case, does "the ontology of representation" really mean? When you try to objectify that ontology as "culture," you are really going back in time to the origins of language, which is, after all, our primary mode of representation. But at that point we automatically assume that language had an origin, something for which we have no evidence, so we find ourselves imagining artifacts instead—like, for instance, sound-combinations coded into words, or perhaps human gestures and motives that were the proto- of human messaging. And that assumes that language is something very simple, like the exchange of information. But where did the information come from? It is not self-evident in the things and forces of the environment, nor is the environment self-evident to us; human beings, as Sidney Mintz points out, have no natural food—everything we eat we have to make up for ourselves. And we have no natural thought patterns either—everything we think we have to make up for ourselves. And we have no evidence on how we made up language for ourselves, or why anyone in their right mind would do so damn fool a thing. But we have plenty of evidence on how language made people up, served as a miniature small-scale model of their thought and being, and that evidence is found in the meaningful synthesis of metaphor, the fractal division of language by itself. We have evidence on how language anticipates what its synthesizing recombinations will have meant once they have been formed, but no evidence on where those recombinations themselves came from. This repositions the question of language's origins from the past to the future, tells us where language is going rather than where it is coming from.

What are the representational parameters of language and time? Is time an effect of language, or language an effect of time? Time, or temporality, has traditionally been thought of in the context of naturalistic regularities and cosmological principles, but all the evidence that this might be true has been accessed and conceptualized by means of language, whereas language, of course, is taken for granted as a product of human ingenuity. But what if the reverse of this were true, and the two are merely coincident features of another representational ontology that we have yet to discover?

Friedrich Nietzsche was what was called in his time a philologist, a student of the ontological roots of representation. His views on the matter, recorded in *The use and abuse of history*, take very little for granted:

> It is a matter for wonder: the moment that is here and gone, that was nothing before and nothing after, returns like a specter to trouble the quiet of a later moment. A leaf is continually dropping out of the volume of time and fluttering away—and suddenly it flutters back into the man's lap. Then he says "I remember . . ." and envies the beast that forgets at once and sees every moment really die, sink into the night and mist, extinguished forever. The beast lives unhistorically; for it "goes into" the present, like a number, without leaving any curious remainder. (Nietzsche [1874] 1949: 5)

What we think of as "time" is limited by the chiasmatic nature of our own familiarity with it. As an antitwin function (cf. chapter 1), it is an extension of the double-proportional constitution of the human phenomenon, and it reapportions our temporal experiences in accordance with that model. As always in cases where chiasmatic double proportioning is involved, there is a subject/ object shift implied, incorporating a transposition of ends and means. Thus in Nietzsche's case the double comparison involves the perceptible presence of time, which Henri Bergson called *durée*, or duration, and the objective, measurable passage of time, the "time" of the temporal physicist. If the duration of time is taken to be the end, then the passage of time suffices as the means to that end, whereas if, contrariwise, the passage of time is taken to be the end, as in temporal physics, then the presence, or duration, of time serves as the means to that end. Logically, then, Nietzsche's "moment that is here and gone" and then "returns like a specter to trouble the quiet of a later moment" reduces to a subject/object shift between the presence of time's passage and the passage of time's presence, reiterating the ancient Greek dichotomy of Epimetheus, or "afterthought," and Prometheus, or "forethought," basically the working contrast between convention and invention used extensively in my earlier book *The invention of culture* (1981). In that sense the present work is the logical sequel to the earlier one.

In the broader scheme of things, there are then logically only two kinds of time: *past in its own future, or recollective time*, the "memory" effect, and *future in its own past*, the effect of "innovation."

This brings us to the ontological crux of the matter: just as space depends on miniaturization for its representational edge, its ability to be tangible and manifest as a "thing" in the world, so time depends on comparison and comparatives to have any reality at all. Spatiality is a scalar phenomenon, temporality a vectoral and self-differentiating one: *time is the difference between itself and space; space is the similarity between them.* This effectively precludes any effort, such as that of Einstein and Minkowski, to identify them as parts of a single continuum, a "spacetime."

There can be no question but that space and time represent tangible properties of the real world around us, but they exist in that way only in the manner in which we accommodate them through our own perception and experience. And that in turn raises the question of whether we represent ourselves to them or they represent themselves through us. That makes the mode of representation crucial to our question: is it unilateral or reciprocal?

What we have learned so far suggests that if this particular question is asked in exactly the right way, it will answer itself. Fortunately, it turns out that the Daribi people of Papua New Guinea have a mode of qualitative/quantitative representation that is the exact analogue of the chiasmatic "double focus" envisioning system of the Barok (*mara*), as well as the bipolar Malaysian *latah* syndrome. The Daribi version takes the form of a uniquely self-reflexive form of binary notation called *sidari-si*, literally "the two-together two," a chiasmatic numbering system that dominates their whole mode of counting and representing number. Like the Asian *yin-yang*, it both grounds itself as a figure and figures itself as the ground of that figure, a mutual integration of singularity and duality that might be represented as the one of two and the two of one. The number is a shifter or self-transformational representor, a self-effecting actuator of the transposition of ends and means. It is the very paradoxical nature of this form of self-representation that prompted Nietzsche to call it "a monistic dialectic." But perhaps the term used in chapter 1 to represent the Mayan Long Count Calendar, binary involution, furnishes the best representation of its conciseness.

Binary involution, of course, is just exactly what is going on in a double-proportional comparison, collapsing what would otherwise be understood as a self-indexing statement (e.g., one that "points to itself"), like "the order of chaos is the chaos of order," into a logical paradox. Logically, so to speak, it is truth divided by itself.

As everyone knows, a true or mathematical holography, a "perfect mutual occlusion of part and whole in any human contingency" (Wagner 2001: 253), is impossible to represent by any means, human or otherwise. Understood in chiasmatic terms, however, via the mutual figure–ground reversal ("transposition") of ends and means, the problem of holographic representation executes what Martin Holbraad and Morten Axel Pedersen (2017) would call an "ontological turn": *the very fact that we cannot represent a true holography means that a true holography can and does represent us.* The inherently holographic obviation figure with its implicit self-abnegation in the form of an event horizon corresponds to a default after-image of our inability to represent holographic reality. It is in essence what Victor Turner would call an antistructure, not a "deconstruction," whatever that might mean, but a total negation, a negative imprint of anything that one might identify with construction.

An obviation figure is in other words a triasmus, if the term be allowed, a chiasmus divided by itself. The obviation figure is based on a device of fractal mathematics called the Sierpinski grid, and fractality works on self-division rather than multiplication. An obviation figure divides itself by itself and keeps on dividing itself by itself until there is nothing left but an event horizon.

Metaphor, like obviation, is language divided by itself. It is what Carlos Castaneda (1987) calls "silent knowledge"—an image of language in the language of image. Thus a metaphor is all about what it does not mean: it has no subject, and is therefore silent on the matter of subjectivity. It is a prime example of the antistructural medium that Victor Turner calls "liminality."

Thus if one can think of an obviational sequence as the extensional form of a metaphor—"metaphor spread out" (Wagner 1986), the metaphor of a metaphor of a metaphor—it can be understood as a protracted search for the subject it does not have ("desperately seeking subject"), a cumulative desubjection of language to the point of no return, approximating to the event horizon of a black hole.

From this we can conclude that metaphor, antistructure, and energy share the same description, and can be used interchangeably for that reason (no subject, no objection). All three are invisible to the unpracticed eye, and must be inferred from their effects on other things, like a quantum singularity. The fact that our whole concept of energy is an exercise in self-deception, that there are no specific kinds of energy other than the "kind" of its conversion from one state to another, reviewed in chapter 1 as an evidence of the reciprocity of perspectives, now leads to an even more profound and astonishing conclusion. This is that energy itself is not a natural fact at all, but an effect of our cognitive apperception of the world around us. There is no one kind of energy, or metaphor, or antistructure but that it needs "another kind" in order to be perceived in the transformational terms that are proper to it. Thus when we look at a star in the

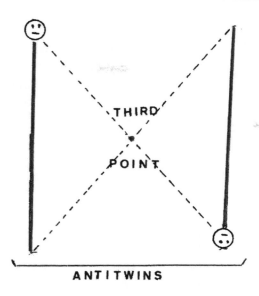

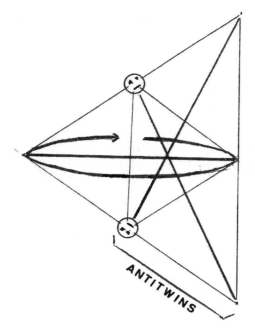

Triasmus

sky, what we actually perceive is not the photons emitted by the celestial object itself, but the neuronic energy of the optic nerve that converts that light into a form that makes sense to our perception. In other words, we see ourselves seeing the star, but never see the real star at all, and in the same way we know ourselves knowing, and understand ourselves understanding, exactly as it should be if Leibniz's posited entelechy were true. We perceive the reflection of our own thoughts on the inner surface of the monad.

But this still leaves us with a question: what is antistructure, and why is obviation an exemplary representation of it? First of all, obviation is a miniature small-scale model of a true, mathematical holographic distribution, something totally different from anything one might imagine, that takes form, as noted above, only through our inability to imagine it. Less cryptically, it defines itself inadvertently to our inability to define it, and in that way amounts to a mirror-image of the searching intellect.

Why is the obviation device a self-modeling image of itself, and what is meant by "self-imaging" in this contingency? The device is self-symmetrical, the image of an image imaging itself, focusing the six metaphors formed at the apices of the two inverted intersecting triangles into a single, compound image that is at once the picture of its formation and its demise. This means that the obviation, like a symphony about to be performed or a tale about to be told, is all there at once, regardless of the order of performance or narration, and that its self-modeling is a static feature, regardless of the dynamics of one's understanding of it. This recalls Zuckerkandl's observation, in *Man the musician*, that "a work of music grows in a dimension that is perpendicular to time" (1973: 191).

Otherwise, the classic example of the self-modeling phenomenon comes from Goethe's researches into the interrelationships of plant species. He called it the *Urpflantz* ("primal plant"), and explained that the type was neither the first plant nor the most recent one to appear, but the one that is just exactly in the middle, the archetype upon which all the other species of plants are modeled. The biological species itself, *Cordiline terminalis*, has a widespread distribution in the equatorial regions of the world (Goethe identified it in Sicily), and is used in decorative planting in gardens and hotel lobbies. Its striking feature is that it buds out of itself in all aspects of its growth and development, keeping the same convulvular patterning of leaf and stem, as though it were mimicking the heliacal configuration of its own DNA.

What role does automimesis play in the understanding of entelechy? Each individual monad is a microcosm of the entelechy that contains them all, and holography means that entelechy itself is a macrocosm of all the individual monads. There is a part/whole identity (not a relation) at work here, and that identity resonates equivocally among them. They are in that respect like tuning forks or crystals that resonate all together at once without there being any physical connection between them. Thus it is permissible, as Leibniz himself did, to call the individual monads themselves "entelechies," for their holographic resonance makes their integrity and tensegrity (identity with one another) into one and the same thing.

Entelechy = holographic resonance, the term "resonance" being used here in a synaesthetic sense, one that transcends the boundaries and separate domains of the five senses. Hence "resonance," in this usage, refers to infinite self-replication in an abstract or mathematical sense, a self-unifying vibration. To demonstrate what I mean by this, I shall follow the precedent set by Claude Lévi-Strauss in his *Mythologiques* series (1971), and draw my example from music. What role does resonance play in the formal, or audible, composition of a work of music? An astute critic once pointed out that most composers begin a major work with a small set of related themes, and generate the motion (kinaesthesia) of the music from the interaction of those themes. In the case of certain composers, such as Bartók and Sibelius, however, the opposite of this procedure takes place, and the themes themselves are generated by the movement of the orchestra. In that case the thematic material itself is the result of a resonant inspiration. (I suggest Bartók's Music for Strings, Percussion, and Celesta and Sibelius's Fourth Symphony for comparison: in resonantial terms they are practically the same piece.)

Lest this seem a trivial example to the reader, I shall broaden my perspective and compare two separate traditions: the classic raga tradition of India and the symphonic tradition of Euro-America. In the raga tradition what one might regard as "themes" are barely recognizable as such, and form part of an ever-changing improvisatory resonance, as in jazz, whereas in the Western case the studied appearance and reappearance of the thematic punctuates the formal structure of the music. Hence the Western symphonic tradition interprets the temporal progression of the music as though it were a message, with something to say, whereas the raga tradition, like the music of Bartók and Sibelius, obviates it. (It is noteworthy that Sibelius actually used explicitly holographic examples in discussing the composition of his work [Wagner 2001: 156].)

As against double-proportional comparisons, as inventoried in the first two chapters of this text, obviation uses a third-point perspective, and runs its course in a sequence of part/whole comparatives. The contrast, which makes all the difference in the world, should be clear to the reader by now. Chiasmatic, or double-proportional comparatives, are limited in range and scope by their own self-constituting internal polarization to go just so far and no further, whereas part/whole comparatives engage and transmute the totality of the perspective at every point. They comment on the whole rather than themselves. As evidenced in the fractal imagery of the Sierpinski grid, obviation is based on the close comparison of interested triangular forms, identified and contrasted in such a way as to correspond to the changes in overall perspective afforded by the (metaphoric) substitutions that trace out its analytical exegesis.

From this point of view, a de facto double-proportional comparison forms the initial point of departure for any obviational sequence, just exactly as in Lévi-Strauss's Canonic Formula for Myth. In ontological terms, however, every representation implies a double-proportional comparison with the reality of representation itself, whether this be actual or imaginary. In other words the thing we call, for want of a better term, "the imagination" takes on the role of subject and objects at once, like the silhouetted human hand in the Iberian cave paintings. The imagination imagines itself as a necessary precondition of its agency, copies itself upon itself and so disguises its role. Thus Hamlet, in the play of that name, fancies himself an actor (enacting himself) when he engages the traveling players, Rembrandt depicted himself as one of the crucifiers of Christ in a crucifixion scene, and Jan Vermeer shows his back to the viewer in *The artist in his studio*, revealing in a sort of visual code that he used a camera obscura as his painting technique—a type of projection that inverts the front and back of the scene. In these three examples, reality is represented as the unreality it represents, like the silhouetted hand in the cave. Representation is a two-edged sword.

And obviation, to prove its point, adds a third edge, as though to remind us that the cave-hand is cut off at the wrist; there are three rather than two crosscutting polarities (axes of cancellation), corresponding to the triangular or trinitarian format, and the tension between reality and representation disappears into the oblivion of the event horizon.

TO *BEE* OR NOT TO *BEE*

Ontology is a Hamlet-question: "To be or not to be," and in this case the question it asks is as old as the Paleolithic cave art itself: is representation a reality of life itself, or is reality itself merely a form of representation? If the latter, then the animals depicted on the cave walls will appear as if by magic in the space outside of the cave, and if the former, then the very first French impressionists will appear within the cave, as if by design. In other words the real question here is that of whether obviation is a real thing that happens in the real world, or merely something that could be represented in any of a number of different ways.

What makes a play or political drama distinctive is that a double-proportional comparison of this sort establishes the dramaturgical arena and sets the tone for all that is to follow. Plot and counterplot "double cross" each other, as in the subplot of Gloucester in *King Lear*, or the twisted fates of Laertes and Prince Hamlet in Shakespeare's play of *Hamlet*. The idea of a play or drama copying itself, "modeling itself upon itself," is, so to speak, "folded" within the very concept of Shakespeare's play. The play "plays" itself, both in a literal and a figurative sense; every time Hamlet is staged in a new context it is to a different purpose, with different actors, a different glance of humanity into the mirror of itself.

How does the play of *Hamlet* copy itself upon itself? Let me parse this out in terms of what we might like to call "autokinesis." The secret of staging a drama has almost nothing to do with the standard assumptions about "telling the story," of reenacting a narrative event-structure as it may have happened in the real world. The secret of obviation is that it combines the otherwise separate logics of nonlinear causality, double-proportional comparison, self-modeling, and part/whole comparison altogether as though they were one thing with a singular logic of its own—a logic that is itself the tale of its own coming into being. As if the final consummation of a subject were at one and the same time the point of its origination.

How does Shakespeare's play of *Hamlet* copy itself on itself? Let me break it down into "stages":

A. Hamlet plays Hamlet. Deprived by treachery of his right to succeed his father as king of Denmark, Prince Hamlet the decision to "act himself mad."
B. Polonius plays "father": Polonius, the court councillor, advises his own son, Laertes, "To thine own self be true," thereby contradicting Hamlet's decision to act himself mad. (Like all court councillors, and most psychiatrists, Polonius substitutes platitudes for wisdom.)

C. Hamlet plays dumb. Deprived of his opportunity to play himself in spite of himself instead of playing his father because of his father, Prince Hamlet decides to abolish language altogether and stage a redux of his father's murder as a "dumb show," an unspeaking "play within a play" (play plays play).

D. Laertes plays Hamlet. While accosting his mother with accusations of incest, Hamlet "accidentally" stabs Polonius, thinking him Claudius, and thus doing exactly the same thing to Laertes and Ophelia that Claudius had done to him: kills their father (parricide plays parricide).

E. Claudius plays Laertes. Now it is Claudius and Laertes, as allies, who play Prince Hamlet's role in reverse, seeking to avenge Hamlet's "accidental" murder of Polonius by staging a "smart" (e.g., "not so dumb") show, a duel on the boards. (By killing their father for whatever reason, Hamlet obviates his relationships with his best friend Laertes, and his fiancée, Ophelia.)

F. Fortinbras plays Hamlet, stages his own "even smarter than smart" show by supplanting the whole Elsinore court and incorporating Denmark into a union with his own Norway. (Chalk up another one for the Normans.)

"The one in the mirror borrows the action of parricide to kill itself." Viewed in terms of the third-point perspective, the Hamlet motif has three significant axes that determine its self-modeling energy configuration, a configuration that remains the same regardless of which "Hamlet" one is looking at. These axes are indicated in the illustration below as A–D, the "axis of sanity," B–E, the "axis of language and relationship," and C–F, the "axis of containment." Taken together, they illustrate the crucial and determinate role of nonlinear causality in the employment of the obviation itself. Suppose we begin at the beginning, point A, and join the action as it ensues. The apparition of the elder Hamlet's ghost puts Prince Hamlet in an unenviable position: regardless of whether he "believes in" ghosts or not, his honor as a royal heir positively demands that he relay his father's message to the court. But his honor as a member of that court also demands that he watch his tongue and that he should not utter charges, however true, that might threaten the subversion of the new ruler, his uncle Claudius. Thus he takes the decision to "act himself mad," give the impression of irresponsibility in his speech so that his words will be disqualified as those of a madman. Though he does succeed in this, its whole purport puts him in immediate conflict with the position of the court advisor (national insecurity advisor?) Polonius, whose maxim "To thine own self be true" serves as the moral watchword for the whole play. Thus, in turn, B–E, the axis of language and relationship, opaques Hamlet's "mad act" and makes it necessary for him to avoid the use of language altogether in presenting his father's message to the court. Hence he stages that message in the form of a "dumb show" or mime—a purely mimetic stage play with no words allowed, a "play within the play" or containment (axis C–F) of the message within the very medium in which the larger play is offered to the court.

Thus when we come to the point of closure of the "sanity" axis, at D, Hamlet's inadvertent stabbing of Polonius through the arras, or curtain, in his mother's chambers is hardly an accident in terms of the energy signature of the obviation itself. For it was because of Polonius's banal "To thine own self be true" pseudo-morality that Hamlet's covert dumb show message succeeded all too well, and led him to believe that it was Claudius, rather than Polonius, who was spying on him in his mother's room. So the termination of the sanity axis (A–E) is an irony that proves Hamlet to be truly insane after all, for what sane man would murder his own future father-in-law, driving his betrothed, Ophelia, to madness and suicide, and doing to his best friend, Laertes, just exactly what his uncle Claudius had done to him (killed his father)?

A weasel like Claudius is going to take immediate advantage of this, and turn the plot around on itself. On the flip side of the B–E "axis of language and relationship" reversal, Hamlet's uncle, the king, arranges a purely adventitious alliance with his victim's victim ("the enemy of my enemy is my ally"), and plans and stages a virtual "play without the play," a classic courtly "duel on the boards" between Laertes and Hamlet. Of course they poison each other with their blades, and get Gertrude, Hamlet's mother, into the bargain (no curtains this time), but Claudius was not counting on the triangulation effect of parallax—the fact that Laertes, as third party, has enough critical distance to make out the shape of what is truly going on—something that neither Claudius nor Hamlet could have done unaided. "*The king! Kill the king!*" Laertes shouts,[1] and Hamlet, with his last strength, goes and does so.

This sets up the requital of the final and conclusive axial inversion—the obviation of the plot itself. The reflex of F–C, the axis of containment. For just

---

1. *Editor's note.* Laertes actually says "the king, the king's to blame" (*Hamlet*, Act V, Scene II).

as the synthesis at C, the "play within the play," or mute pantomime faking murder, was the follow-up on Hamlet's giving up on language, so the action of Norway's Prince Fortinbras at F is the follow-up on Claudius's bloody "play without a play," for Fortinbras brings his army up and contains the entire state of Denmark, Elsinore included. From his majestically indifferent point of view, Elsinore just tore itself to pieces, and he walked in and picked them up. If murder were sex, this would be royal incest.

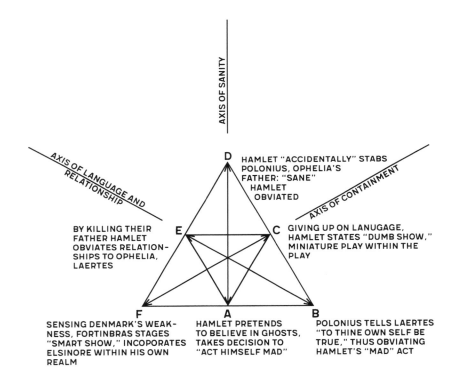

Denmark: Royal incest

But if incest is what happens when the forces of reproduction are turned inward against one another, what would outcest be? Is it possible that incest and outcest share the same energy-signature? The term "outcest" is virtually unknown in the anthropological literature, but natural-world analogues are not hard to find. The behavioral phenomenon known to bee-keepers as "swarming" is a case in point; it is a natural part of the apiary life-cycle, and probably millions of years old. As an amateur beekeeper living in the Virginia countryside, I was able to observe the process and effectively "hive the swarm" in the early summer of 1978. Unbeknownst to me at the time, the whole process "stages" itself, using the same self-modeling strategy as the play of *Hamlet*, so we might provisionally entitle the play of analogies between the two "To *bee* or not to *bee*."

We have by now some reliable, objective evidence on the particulars of communication (and therefore relationship, if that is the word) among bees, but nothing but innuendo to go on when it comes to consciousness, rendering such terms as "intersubjectivity" particularly odious. Nonetheless, and drawing upon innuendo if nothing else, it appears that at certain times, perhaps for reasons that biologists would ascribe to hormones or pheromones, a small group of worker bees begin to act very strangely, and, acting in concert, begin to feed a substance called "royal jelly" to an otherwise anonymous larva in its cell. They "act themselves mad," so to speak, for such subversion of royal authority is normally a lethal offense (A–D, axis of sanity), for a sustained diet of royal jelly is all that is needed to transform a normally sterile worker larva into an egg-producing, hive-reproducing queen. Furthermore, since a hive cannot abide two queens at the same time, they must proceed in secret (point B, controverting Polonius: "To thine own state be false"). Hence what the rogue workers are producing is what is known on Broadway as a "closet queen" or a "drag queen." Point C (synthesis): "hive within the hive." Just as Prince Hamlet used a pantomime, a "play within a play," to "catch the conscience of the king," so the rogue workers set up a revolutionary "party cell." Thus, as in Hamlet's case, the whole "falling action" (pragmatic afterlife) of the drama is set up at point D by a sudden "out of the closet" disclosure: the new queen emerges as a public fact, "to post with such dexterity to incestuous sheets!" (in this case sheets of honeycomb). As in Hamlet's case (point E, resolution of E–B axis, "twist of the knife in the gut," as my Mythodology students would have it), this leads to a duel on the boards between the two rival monarchs and their factions, (quite literally so, in my case, since my beehive was resting on boards). Inevitably, and we know of no exceptions to this, the new queen's party triumphs over the old, and the hive as a whole is outcested, decontained from within.

What are we to make of this? The fact that Shakespeare's play of *Hamlet* has what an earlier generation of anthropologists would call a "cultural" agenda, and the swarming of a beehive a "natural" one, has little to do with the powerful analogic ontology that makes each seem a mimetic copy of the other. For that

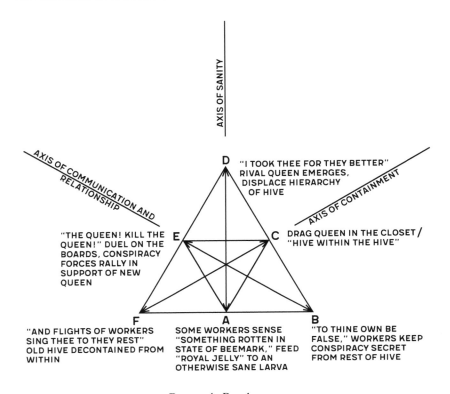

Bee-mark: Royal outcest

ontology is neither natural nor cultural, but based on the same universal logic as the cosmos itself is. It is the mirror-reflection of entelechy.

THE ONE YOU SEE IN INFINITY'S MIRROR

Imagine an infinite intelligence, the better part of whose understanding is obsessed with the possibility that anything like finitude might exist. Now imagine the opposite: a being of finite intelligence and lifespan obsessed with trying to gauge the paradoxical mind-puzzle of infinity. What are the differences between the two? Each must borrow the other's viewpoint to know itself by contrast to its opposite, for Wittgenstein reminds us that the eye is never within its own field of vision.

Hence the problem of limits, boundaries, and discrete knowledge parameters, of the limited and limitless, resolves itself into one of means and extremes, and so betrays itself as yet another disguise of the double-proportional comparison, and all the variant forms of it, like the quadratic equation, the self-modeling proposition, etc., another example of second-attention pseudo-mysticism. The problem is not merely self-reflexive, it is insoluble. It is like extracting the negative square root of $E = mc^2$, or like asking one of those apocryphal UFO space aliens where it came from, and then pretending to be surprised at its reply: "Actually, I forgot." Entelechy carries its own universe along with it.

Epilogue
Totality viewed in the imagination

Lest the reader find themselves perplexed by the changes and sudden reidentifications of operant value in the subjects at hand in this text—subject/object shift, figure–ground reversal, transposition of ends and means, etc.—that occur throughout this text, I should like to add a clarification. To be sure, all of these operant forms are variant objectifications of the main subject of the first chapter, the reciprocity of perspectives. But there is a danger here: without going into specifics we run the hazard of missing the basic unity of the subject under consideration.

A shift from subject to object, or vice versa, in a discourse of logical disquisition is commonplace enough, and we perform it countless times each day without taking special notice of it. But the fact that any one or another of these chiasmatic breaks in any given context is the means of qualifying another, and vice versa, is taken for granted as the logical function of syntax itself. Consider, for instance, the curious relation between metaphor and humor.

A metaphor has no subject; it is all about what it does not mean; it is like a bolt of lightning that has already run its course by the time you notice it, so that all you really know of it is the afterimage. Is humor a liminality of laughing at one's ability to laugh, a kind of self-imitative hysteria? What is the logical relation of humor to the liminality of metaphor? It is very simple: humor reverses the order of cause and effect, in the way that a joke presents one with the effect first, and then surprises one in the punchline with a "cause" one never expected.

Thus if metaphor has no subject, and humor, by default, has no object, the difference between them is a subject/object shift or transposition of ends and means, and thus by definition nonlinear. Surprisingly enough for a quality with such a chimerical profile, the liminality (Victor Turner's term) between a subject without an object and an object without a subject does have a logical infrastructure, one that it shares with such other difficult-to-grasp objectifications as time, energy, and order. All of these are examples of chiasmatic syllogistics, like Wittgenstein's Propositions or Gödel's Proof. Let me illustrate: chiasmus is the derivative of what logicians call a double-proportional comparison: two things are compared with each other twice, and in reverse order the second time. Thus in terms of the present discussion one might say that metaphor takes itself as a subject in the way that humor takes itself as an object (e.g., "objects" to itself), and that for that reason these two forms of chiasmatic liminality are coconspirators in a self-symmetrical analogical syllogism, a cross-comparison between the subjectless object and the objectless subject: the metaphor of humor and the humor of metaphor.

Metaphor has no subject; its object, so to speak, is the means of its own expression (hence *meta*, "means," and *phor*, "bearing"), and thus in this case ends = means. Humor, by contrast, has no object, in the sense that its means or cause is a transposition of the sequentially defined cause-and-effect sequence. Thus, as we have seen, metaphor and humor are chiasmatic twins of one another, alternative facies of a double-proportional comparison. How does "funny" compare with "fantasy"? In this case, the four terms of the double comparison are difference, similarity, ends, and means. Metaphor has no subject because it is elicited by the similarity between ends and means; humor has no object because it is elicited by the difference between ends and means, which are transposed in its expression so as to enhance their differentiation. Putting the two together, we can derive a self-modeling syllogism, or format for chiasmatic expression, one that models the subject/object shift and the transposition of ends and means upon one another: humor is the difference between *itself* and metaphor; metaphor is the similarity between them. (In other words a joke is always metaphoric, but a metaphor is not necessarily humorous.)

Humor, then, is "funny" because it depends for its effect on a self-differentiating variable (e.g., the difference that differs from itself), which, because of its indeterminacy, cannot be predicated. In metaphor, however, this quality of self-differentiation is accorded to language itself, as in the observation that "metaphor is language's way of trying to figure out what we mean by it" (Wagner 2001: 253). Self-differentiation is the wild card in the deck, the power stroke, so to speak. It is in this sense of language's ability, as a self-determining variable, to speak of us more lucidly than we are able to speak it that prompted Carlos Castaneda to identify chiasmatic logic as "heightened awareness" or "the second attention," and Victor Turner to write that ritual is "expressing what cannot be thought of, in view of thought's subjugation to essences" (1975: 187). It is likewise echoed in Ludwig Wittgenstein's Proposition 4.121: "What finds its reflection in language, language cannot represent" (1961).

Whether one thinks of it as a separate "attention" or not, chiasmatic logic constitutes a separate and distinctive sphere of human achievement and understanding. What we call "civilization" presents a special case of this, for in that case its parameters are guaranteed and protected by professional ethics and a hierarchical institutionalized base.

Subliminally speaking, Castaneda's overmystified understanding of the second attention, which is the central mystery in all of his books (including the brilliant *The art of dreaming*, 1993) represents exactly the same self-differentiating factor, in exactly the same way, as Immanuel Kant's ontology of the noumenal and the phenomenal. Kant: "The noumenal is the difference between *itself* and the phenomenal; the phenomenal is the similarity between them." Compare Castaneda: "The *nagual* [e.g., noumenon] is the difference between *itself* and the *tonal* [e.g., phenomenon]; the *tonal* is the similarity between them."[1] After explaining this "sorcerer's explanation," as he calls it, to Castaneda in simplified (nonchiasmatic) terms, don Juan tells him that he will never be able to understand it (most likely because he did not himself). What a pity! Perhaps Castaneda should have apprenticed himself to Kurt Gödel instead.

It is important in understanding all of this that one cannot think in the second attention. At best one skirts the boundaries of what "thinking" would have to imply, takes what could be called the "analogical derivative" of the subject that would otherwise have to be thought through in words. What we normally call "thinking" is actually a process of rationalization, using words and above all syntax to articulate in literal terms what analogy discards as trivial. An analogy "thinks by itself," in its own terms, figures out what rationalization could only "figure in": the ends of rationalization are the means of analogy.

If every great civilization can be seen to have written its power-signature in the specific form of chiasmatic expression that suits its purpose, then it should be no surprise that ours should take the form of automation, the one that

---

1.   *Editor's note.* The author did not provide source details for these two quotes and we have been unable to locate them.

"works." Unlike the second attention of the Mexican civilization, or the suave deception of the Hindu *Indrajal* ("Indra-net"; cf. Wagner 2001), automation is a technological application, like the wheel.

This does not, however, disqualify it from introspective profundity. Their commonplace wheel, for example, is a chiasmatic prodigy—a perfect self-modeling of the double-proportional comparison in physical terms. As we noted in chapter 1, no matter how you divide it into halves, one half of a moving wheel always goes in a direction opposite to that of the other half, but with exactly the same speed and momentum. But the physical chiasmus is not limited to moving objects; in the case of the Möbius strip and the Klein bottle, a special branch of mathematics called "topology" had to be invented to incorporate its counterintuitive features within the commonplace measures of geometry. Static exemplars of the classic yin/yang chiasmus, they project a constitutive motion that can only be experienced in the imagination of the viewer. The Möbius strip and the Klein bottle are respectively chiasmatic inversions of one another: the Möbius strip contains its own laterality (sidedness) within its single-sidedness, and vice versa, whereas the Klein bottle simultaneously contains its own decontainment and decontains its containment. In a sublime representation of the reciprocity of perspectives, both figures are divided by the analogy that unites them and united by the distinction that separates them.

Who would guess that this is the same principle as automation? Although it has transformed our world in multiple ways, automation is neither a means to an end nor an end in itself, being both at the same time. Hence its most prodigious products, like powered flight, the computer, or the automobile, are less "tools" or resources than they are self-fulfilling prophecies. The internet, for instance, contains no messages that are not, either directly or indirectly, about itself. The medium, so to speak, is always the message.

All of these issues have been compounded together under the rubric of "artificial intelligence" or automated thought. The big problem is originality. It is not simply that an intrinsically derivative process has been substituted for a more original one and called by its name, but rather that cyberspace has secured a patent on the originality stereotype, and reduced it to the status of a logo, or trademark. Will future ages transpose the ends and means of this and conclude that we were originally invented by our machines?

The ubiquity of automation calls to mind the question of whether the chiasmatic relation is projected by human beings upon the world around them, or projected backward by nature upon human beings. Of course, the question itself is a case in point, for, being of a chiasmatic nature (e.g., reflecting back on itself), it is both answered in the asking of it and asked in the answering. It is our antitwin. As pointed out in chapter 1, the four-term double-proportional comparison that determines the disposition of gender and laterality in the human race, can be viewed alternatively from a natural or cultural perspective. Viewed from the physical perspective (gender twinned outward, laterality inward), we appear as a race of bigendered, bilaterally symmetrical beings. Viewed from the cultural side—gender twinned inward (incest) and lateral extension (the basis of technology) twinned outward—we emerge as a race made conscious of its own kin connections (kinship as avoidance of incest), and capable of technologically altering the world around it through technology, an "auto-mated," so to speak, *Homo chiasmaticus*. In this case there can be no question of the evolutionary step that led to human sentience.

The next step, the one that takes us beyond chiasmus, is the logic of happening itself: nonlinear causality, or what the medievals called "the wheel of fortune."

In effect, the question that is answered in its asking and asked in its answering is neither here nor there. The chiasmus of a chiasmus is like a 360-degree turn, and takes you right back to the starting point. But the chiasmus of a chiasmus *of* a chiasmus, based on three consecutive turns, is how obviation happens to itself—divides the 360-degree turn by another half-turn. More simply put, it carries the chiasmatic relation through to its ultimate self-negation, which is why the term "obviation" is most appropriate here. Thus, although the self-reversible double-proportional comparison relies on four terms, obviation depends on six. For instance, in the expression quoted in chapter 4 ("third-point perspective"), "The one in the mirror borrows the action of looking to see itself" (Wagner 2001: 234), we can discriminate three consecutive oppositional pairs ($3 \times 2 = 6$), hence: (1) self versus other, (2) perception versus deception, and (3) verification versus falsification. Translated into logical terms, what this means is that the person imaged in the mirror (other) has obviated (falsified) the one looking into it.

Obviation is then the completive or consummative form of chiasmatic logic: instead of a double-proportional comparison it is a triple-proportional noncomparison, a triasmus, so to speak (echoing the medical term "triage"). The idea of obviation is self-manifesting and self-realizing, like a chiasmatic transpositioning of ends and means: it is both a technique for analyzing a subject, and the ontology, so to speak, of the subject so studied.

Thus obviation, as a self-modeling process, is a way of coming into being and going out of being at the same time, like the astronomical black hole. The verb "to obviate" is simultaneously transitive and intransitive, and in this sense is the very essence of ontology itself. It is for this reason that buzzwords like "construction" and "deconstruction" are irrelevant in this context, for obviation is in those terms self-instrumental.

It is precisely because a metaphor has no subject that a self-modeling sequence that is made of nothing but metaphors—the metaphor of a metaphor of a metaphor, so to speak—closes in upon itself (obviates) in a final demonstration that it is its own subject, a symbol that stands for itself. Understood in this way that it is the cumulative or extensional (e.g., spread out in space) form of metaphor, it is a process of continual self-imaging that builds to a point of self-abnegation, recalling the shrewd observation of the Japanese sage Dogen that "what is happening here and now is obstructed by happening itself; it has sprung free from the brains of happening." It is a joke played on life itself, like the medieval "wheel of fortune"—*totes ces vu imagine*, "totality viewed in the imagination," that was presented as an analogy for obviation by the medieval master-architect Villard d'Honnecourt (see diagram, next page).

The "wheel of fortune," with its unavoidable, unconscionable ups and downs—why is the transposition of ends and means, with its necessary inversion of the subject being studied and the means by which it is studied, an aspect of the self-modeling that is inherent in the chiasmatic profile of the human constitution? The reader will recall the necessary inversion of physical versus cultural ends and means in the distinctively human antitwinning configuration: gender twinned outward and laterality twinned inward versus gender twinned inward and laterality outward: the physical and the cultural sides of the double comparison serve in each case as the means to the other's ends. In effect, then, the same chiasmatic relation obtains between the two contrasting elevations as within each of them, forming a part/whole relation that repeats itself within itself (Wagner 2001 calls this the "human hologram").

If the obviation sequence, with its motif of perfect holographic convergence, mirrored in any conceivable way, provides the best possible model of a self-modeling totality, then one has a perfect right to challenge Wittgenstein's conclusions about the significance of the *Tractatus*. For if it is true that the document "proves nothing" or is completely meaningless, those observations only substantiate the fact that the work as a whole is an obviation of its own purpose, a "symbol that stands for itself." In other words, it depends on nothing outside of itself, and, as a self-modeling discourse, obviates its own message about itself.

Totes ces vu imagene, "Totality viewed in the imagination"; the Device of Obviation drawn by the greatest gothic cathedral architect of all, Villard d'Honnecourt
(c. 1225–50), in the shape of the medieval "wheel of fortune," possibly as an imaginative
design for a rose window. Notice the accuracy with which d'Honnecourt has captured
(a) the three axes of cancellation and (b) the six basic substitutions. Note also the sub-
tlety by which he conserved the basic triangular design in drawing the human figures.
Did d'Honnecourt, designer of the Notre Dame and Chartres cathedrals, also draw in
the figure–ground reversal by which the age of modern science succeeded that of the
Holy Sacrament at about the time of the Reformation? Roughly contemporary with the
Mayan *Hunab Ku* autoglyph, "The One and Only God," which appeared in Yucatán.

Why is this important? It is important because the technique of the projective hologram was invented (by Dennis Gabor, who received the Nobel Prize for it) some years after Wittgenstein had abandoned philosophy. In essence, then, Wittgenstein would have no accurate idea of what "holography" means, lacking a practical demonstration of it. The philosophical sense of the concept plays no part in any world civilization, saving that of India, though the ancient Irish Book of Kells is replete with holographic images.

Holographic self-correspondence is neither voluntary nor involuntary in nature, but instead is motivated by a third-party neurological nexus called the parasympathetic nervous system. Not surprisingly, the parasympathetic is formed gradually over the lifespan of the individual by a set of chiasmatic correspondences between the voluntary and involuntary systems, an ontological learning curve, as it were. Occasionally, under the very happiest circumstances, the whole thing crystallizes into a synthesis by means of a holographic projection of the self (Castaneda calls this "burning with the fire from within"), a condition sometimes confused with the absurd notion of "spontaneous combustion in human beings."

References

Bakhtin, Mikhail. 1981. "Forms of Time and of the Chronotope in the Novel: Notes toward a Historical Poetics." In *The dialogic imagination: Four essays*, 84–258. Austin: University of Texas Press.

Barth, Fredrik. 1975. *Ritual and knowledge among the Baktaman of New Guinea.* New Haven, CT: Yale University Press.

Bateson, Gregory. 1958. *Naven: A survey of the problems suggested by a composite picture of the culture of a New Guinea tribe drawn from three points of view.* Stanford, CA: Stanford University Press.

———. 1978. *Steps to an ecology of mind: Collected essays in anthropology, psychiatry, evolution, and epistemology.* New York: Ballantine.

Borges, Jorge Luis. 1998. "The garden of forking paths." In *Collected fictions*, 119–28. Translated by Andrew Hurley. New York: Penguin Putnam.

Castaneda, Carlos Arana. 1968. *The teachings of don Juan: A Yaqui way of knowledge.* Berkeley: University of California Press.

———. 1971. *A separate reality: Further conversations with don Juan.* New York: Simon & Schuster.

———. 1975. *Tales of power.* New York; Simon & Schuster.

———. 1987. *The power of silence: Further lessons of don Juan.* New York: Simon & Schuster.

———. 1993. *The art of dreaming.* New York: HarperCollins.

Crook, Tony. 2007. *Exchanging skin: Anthropological knowledge, secrecy and Bolivip, Papua New Guinea.* Oxford: Oxford University Press

Farella, John R. 1984. *The main stalk: A synthesis of Navajo philosophy*. Tucson: University of Arizona Press.

Holbraad, Martin, and Morten Axel Pedersen. 2017. "Analogic anthropology: Wagner's inventions and obviations." In *The ontological turn: An anthropological exposition*, 69–109. Cambridge: Cambridge University Press.

Jones, Barbara A. 1980. "Consuming society: Food and illness among the Faiwol." Doctoral dissertation, University of Virginia.

Kirsch, Stuart. 2006. *Reverse anthropology: Indigenous analysis of social and environmental relations in New Guinea*. Stanford, CA: Stanford University Press.

Lakoff, George, and Mark Johnson. 1980. *Metaphors we live by*. Chicago: University of Chicago Press.

Le Guin, Ursula K. (1969) 2017. *The left hand of darkness*. London: Gollancz.

Leibniz, Gottfried Wilhelm. (1714) 1989. "The principles of philosophy, or, The monadology." In *Philosophical essays*, 213–24. Edited and translated by Roger Ariew and Daniel Garber. Indianapolis, IN: Hackett.

León-Portilla, Miguel. 1963. *Aztec thought and culture: A study of the ancient Nahuatl mind*. Translated by Jack Emory Davis. Norman: University of Oklahoma Press.

Lévi-Strauss, Claude. 1966. *The savage mind*. Chicago: University of Chicago Press.

———. 1971. *Mythologiques*. Paris: Plon.

Maschio, Thomas. 1994. *To remember the faces of the dead: The plenitude of memory in southwestern New Britain*. Madison: University of Wisconsin Press.

Nietzsche, Friedrich W. (1874) 1949. *The use and abuse of history*. Translated by Adrian Collins. New York: The Liberal Arts Press.

Robbins, Joel. 2004. *Becoming sinners: Christianity and moral torment in a Papua New Guinea society*. Berkeley: University of California Press.

Spencer-Brown, G. 1969. *Laws of form*. London: George Allen and Unwin.

Spencer, Oswald. 1928. *The decline of the West*. Vol. 2. *Perspectives of world history*. Translated by Charles Francis Atkinson. New York: Knopf.

Stolze Lima, Tania. 1999. "The two and its multiple: Reflections on perspectivism in a Tupi community." *Ethnos* 61 (4): 107–31.

Talbot, Michael. 1991. *The holographic universe*. New York: HarperCollins.

Thoreau, Henry David. (1851) 1993. *A year in Thoreau's journal: 1851*. With an introduction and notes by H. Daniel Peck. Harmondsworth, UK: Penguin.

Turner, Victor W. 1975. *Revelation and divination in Ndembu ritual*. Ithaca, NY: Cornell University Press.

Wagner, Roy. 1973. *Habu: Innovation of meaning in Daribi religion*. Chicago: University of Chicago Press.

———. 1981. *The invention of culture*. Chicago: University of Chicago Press.

———. 1986. *Symbols that stand for themselves*. Chicago: University of Chicago Press.

———. 2001. *An anthropology of the subject: Holographic worldview in New Guinea and its meaning and significance for the world of anthropology*. Berkeley: University of California Press.

Weiner, James F. 1991. *The empty place: Poetry, space and being among the Foi of Papua New Guinea*. Bloomington: Indiana University Press.

Wittgenstein, Ludwig. 1961. *Tractatus logico-philosophicus*. Translated by D. F. Pears and B. F. McGuinness. London: Routledge & Kegan Paul.

Zuckerkandl, Victor. 1973. *Man the musician*. Vol. 2. *Sound and symbol*. Bollingen Series. Princeton, NJ: Princeton University Press.